THE CLASSIC AMERICAN
QUILT COLLECTION™
◇
WEDDING RING

Edited by
Karen Costello Soltys

 Rodale Press, Emmaus, Pennsylvania

WEDDING RING EDITORIAL STAFF

Editor: *Karen Costello Soltys*

Technical Writer: *Janet Wickell*

Quilt Scout: *Bettina Havig*

Cover and Interior Designer: *Denise M. Shade*

Book Layout: *Tanya L. Lipinski*

Photographer: *Mitch Mandel*

Illustrators: *Mario Ferro and Jackie Walsh*

Copy Editor: *Carolyn Mandarano*

Editorial Assistance: *Stephanie R. Snyder*

Manufacturing Coordinator: *Jodi Schaffer*

RODALE BOOKS

Editorial Director, Home and Garden: *Margaret Lydic Balitas*

Managing Editor, Quilt Books: *Suzanne Nelson*

Art Director, Home and Garden: *Michael Mandarano*

Copy Director, Home and Garden: *Dolores Plikaitis*

Office Manager, Home and Garden: *Karen Earl-Braymer*

Editor-in-Chief: *William Gottlieb*

If you have any questions or comments concerning this book, please write to:
Rodale Press, Inc.
Book Readers' Service
33 East Minor Street
Emmaus, PA 18098

The three-dimensional rose appliqué patterns and techniques on pages 48–49 appear with the permission of Helma Stewart, who first published these patterns in *American Quilter,* Vol. X, Spring 1991.

Library of Congress Cataloging-in-Publication Data

The Classic American quilt collection : wedding ring / edited by Karen Costello Soltys.
p. cm.
ISBN 0–87596–683–7 hardcover
1. Quilting—Patterns. 2. Patchwork—Patterns.
I. Soltys, Karen Costello.
TT835.C593 1995
746.46—dc20 95–7033

Distributed in the book trade by St. Martin's Press

2 4 6 8 10 9 7 5 3 1 hardcover

CONTENTS

Acknowledgments

Plaid Double Wedding Ring, made by Cleo Snuggerud, Sioux Falls, South Dakota. Cleo is the owner of Heirloom Creations, a retail shop that caters to the needs of quilters and needlepointers. She has been quilting for over 20 years. Cleo is a first-generation quilter, but has taught her son to quilt and is currently working on her mother.

Diamond Wedding Ring, made by Joanne Winn, Canton, Ohio. Joanne has been quilting since 1978. She designs and sells quilting patterns under her company name, Canada Goose Designs. Diamond Wedding Ring is just one of her patterns based on circles.

Is This Wedded Bliss?, made by Maureen Carlson, Moline, Illinois. This quilt was shown at the 1994 Quilters' Heritage Celebration in Lancaster, Pennsylvania, and the 1994 International Quilt Festival in Houston, Texas. Maureen loves hand-dyed fabrics, and she dyed the purple fabric for this beauty herself.

Job's Tears, designed and made by Suzzy Chalfant Payne, Fairport, New York, and Susan Aylsworth Bushnell, Doylestown, Pennsylvania, for their book *Creative American Quilting Inspired by the Bible*. In 1976, they developed timesaving methods for making traditional patchwork and authored *Quick and Easy Patchwork on the Sewing Machine* and *Quick and Easy Giant Dahlia*. They've presented hundreds of quilting classes and programs. Their quilts have been featured in several magazines, including *Good Housekeeping*.

Hearts and Hands, designed and made by Deborah Bird Timby, Newport, Rhode Island. Debbie made this family keepsake for her parents' fiftieth wedding anniversary. She began seriously quilting in 1978. Debbie likes the designing process best, and her style ranges from country to traditional to contemporary.

Rose Rings, made by Susan Stein, St. Paul, Minnesota. Susan is a prolific quilter, having made hundreds of quilts, wallhangings, and garments since beginning quiltmaking in 1977. She is also the author of *Colorful Angles* and has contributed to several books in the Singer Reference Library.

Crazy Wedding Ring, made by Joanne Winn, Canton, Ohio. This quilt is another of Joanne's circular patterns offered by her pattern company, Canada Goose Designs. This pattern design is known by several other names, such as Tea Leaf, Orange Peel, and Pincushion.

Red-and-White Wedding Ring, owned by Cindy Rennels, Clinton, Oklahoma. Cindy is the proprietor of Cindy's Quilts in Clinton, and she has been collecting and dealing with antique quilts for nine years.

Spiderwebs and Dewdrops, made by Susan Stein, St. Paul, Minnesota. This wallhanging is another of Susan's specialty Double Wedding Ring quilts that combines the traditional with unexpected contemporary embellishments. It also is made with Susan's favorite medium—hand-dyed cotton fabrics.

Feed Sack Wedding Ring, made by Lizzie Stover and owned by her granddaughter, Bertha Rush, Hatfield, Pennsylvania. Bertha is a prolific quilter and a member of the Variable Star Quilters. Feed Sack Wedding Ring was shown at the 1992 Variable Star Quilt Show and in a quilt exhibit sponsored by the Eastern Mennonite Historical Society in 1994–95. Bertha also hand quilts for other people.

Pickled Watermelon, made by Julee Prose, Ottumwa, Iowa. Julee adapted the Pickle Dish variation of the Wedding Ring for her original Pickled Watermelon quilt for the 1989 American Quilter's Society show. This quilt was also featured in the June 1994 issue of *Quilting Today*.

Silver Anniversary, specially designed for the twenty-fifth anniversary of *Quilter's Newsletter Magazine* by Annie Segal, who adapted it from a 1930s pattern, Indian Wedding Ring. This pattern is also very similar to a 1940 *Kansas City Star* pattern. Silver Anniversary was pieced by Penny Wolf and machine quilted by Jonna Castle. The quilt appeared on the cover of the magazine in September 1994 and was displayed at the 1994 International Quilt Festival in Houston, Texas.

INTRODUCTION

Out of the thousands of quilt designs in existence, Wedding Ring is one of the few that could stand alone as an instantly recognizable symbol of American patchwork.
—Bonnie Leman, *Quilter's Newsletter Magazine*, June 1978

For many quilters, it's love at first sight when they see their first Wedding Ring quilt. Few other quilt designs inspire such abiding affection and enjoy such enduring popularity. Perhaps it's because the graceful curves and interlocking rings carry with them the romance and promise of everlasting love. Or maybe it's because this design lends itself so perfectly to scrap quilts, another perennial love of quiltmakers. Or it could be due to the way the colors and fabrics dance around the rings, almost virtually guaranteeing that no matter what colors or fabrics are used, the final quilt will sparkle with personality.

As with so many of our favorite quilt designs, it's impossible to pinpoint when and where the pattern first emerged. It does seem a bit surprising, though, to discover that this uniquely American quilt pattern was only first developed in this century, sometime in the 1920s or 1930s. It seems especially touching that a quilt symbolizing eternal hope and romance should blossom out of the hard times surrounding the Depression.

Whether American quiltmakers were simply ready to move beyond the square and triangular shapes they had mastered to something more challenging or whether the complexity of piecing curves gave them a way to escape thinking about their troubles, it's clear that there was something in this design that caught their fancy. Although times have changed, this love affair with Wedding Ring quilts has not. Over the past 70 years, this circular pattern has been adapted and modified so that now there are even more variations to love.

In this volume, we're pleased to give you a dozen delightful adaptations of this classic pattern, from the very traditional Feed Sack Wedding Ring (page 74), with its interlocking double rings, to Pickled Watermelon (page 80), a unique adaptation of the Pickle Dish variation. Other variations include Job's Tears (page 22), a pattern that technically isn't a wedding ring but a kissing cousin, and Crazy Wedding Ring (page 50), which features crazy-quilting techniques on the Orange Peel, or Tea Leaf, pattern.

We've also featured some smaller projects. If you want to try your hand at piecing a Wedding Ring quilt and have never done it before, it's a lot easier to start out with 9 or 12 rings rather than with a queen- or king-size quilt. (Of course, each pattern gives directions and yardage requirements for making larger sizes, too.) Once you've mastered the art of joining all of the pieces together, you'll be ready to enjoy making any of the larger-size projects you find here.

For each project, you'll find our customary skill-level rating to prepare you for what you may encounter ahead. Please note that the skill levels are assigned solely upon the characteristics of the quilts in this book and not upon all quilts in general. If you compare piecing a Wedding Ring to piecing a Nine Patch, the Nine Patch deserves an easy rating, while a Wedding Ring is definitely more challenging. However, within the group of 12 Wedding Ring quilts in this book, there are definitely some that are easier than others. For all the projects, we've worked extra hard to make sure the directions and diagrams are clear and detailed and won't leave you stranded. Don't be surprised to find that once you jump in, you can't stop with just one Wedding Ring quilt!

Karen Soltys

Karen Costello Soltys

WEDDING RING
PROJECTS

PLAID DOUBLE WEDDING RING

Skill Level: *Intermediate*

*T*he straight lines of woven plaids and stripes may not seem like an obvious match with the graceful curves of the Wedding Ring pattern, yet they work together very well in this cozy rendition of the classic Double Wedding Ring. Cleo Snuggerud stitched this double-size quilt using a technique developed by John Flynn. The directions that follow are for traditional template construction.

BEFORE YOU BEGIN

If this is your first Double Wedding Ring quilt, be sure to read "Wedding Ring Basics," beginning on page 104, before starting the project. Although each pattern in this book contains specific information for its own unique assembly, many aspects of construction are similar from quilt to quilt.

You will need to make templates from pattern pieces A, B, C, D, and E on page 7. For information about making and using templates, see page 116 in "Quiltmaking Basics."

CHOOSING FABRICS

The rings of this quilt are pieced from an assortment of plaids and stripes in mostly subdued colors, but don't be afraid to mix in a few bright colors for pizzazz, as this quiltmaker did. The yardages for the plaids and stripes listed in the Materials chart are an estimate of the total amount required. For best results, buy small cuts of many plaid and striped fabrics until you've accumulated the total number of yards required for your quilt size.

Quilt Sizes		
	Wallhanging	Double (shown)
Finished Quilt Size	52" × 52"	86½" × 86½"
Finished Ring Diameter	17"	17"
Number of Rings	16	49
Number of Pieced Arcs	80	224

Materials		
	Wallhanging	Double
Assorted plaids and stripes	3 yards	8½ yards
Muslin	1⅞ yards	4⅞ yards
Backing	3¼ yards	8⅛ yards
Batting	60" × 60"	95" × 95"
Binding	¾ yard	1 yard

NOTE: *Yardages are based on 44/45-inch-wide fabrics that are at least 42 inches wide after preshrinking.*

The quilt shown was made entirely from woven plaids and stripes, not printed fabrics. The woven designs give the quilt a homespun feel, one that is softer than what would have been achieved with printed plaids.

If you've never worked with woven plaids, you should note that the weave is usually a little looser than that of printed cottons, which means they can fray and shift more easily. Don't let that word of caution prevent you from using woven plaids, however. The result is definitely worth the effort.

To develop your own color scheme for the quilt, photocopy the **Wedding Ring Color Plan** on page 111, and use crayons or colored pencils to experiment with different color arrangements.

3

Cutting Chart

Fabric	Used For	Piece	Number of Pieces	
			Wallhanging	Double
Muslin	Background	A	16	49
	Melons	B	40	112
Assorted plaids and stripes	Connecting wedges	C	80	224
	Outer wedges of arcs	D	80	224
	Outer wedges of arcs	D reverse	80	224
	Inner wedges of arcs	E	320	896

CUTTING

All measurements include ¼-inch seam allowances. Referring to the Cutting Chart, cut the required number of pieces for your quilt size. Each piece was cut with the straight of grain running through its vertical center rather than with the grain aligned with its straight side edge.

Note: Cut and piece one sample ring before cutting all of the fabric for the quilt.

— Sew Easy —

Because woven plaids and stripes may shift, especially when handling small pieces, try misting your pieces with spray starch. This added bit of stiffness will enable you to line up the edges of the fabric pieces and use an assembly line piecing technique.

PIECING THE ARCS

Step 1. Stack the D, D reverse, and E pieces in separate piles. For a scrappy look, mix the plaids and stripes within each pile, then simply pull a piece off the stack when sewing. Begin each pieced arc with a D piece. To the right of it, sew a succession of four E pieces, as shown in **Diagram 1.** End with a D reverse piece. As you sew, be sure pieces

are oriented so that curves arch in the same direction, as shown. Gently press seams to one side, taking care not to stretch the unit. Repeat until you have assembled all the arcs required for your quilt.

Diagram 1

Step 2. Center and sew a pieced arc to one side of each muslin B melon, as shown in **Diagram 2.** Refer to page 107 in "Wedding Ring Basics" for specific information and advice on assembling the curved pieces common to most Wedding Ring quilts. Press seams toward the melons. You will use half of the pieced arcs for this step.

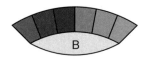

Diagram 2

Step 3. Sew a plaid C piece to each end of the remaining arcs, as shown in **Diagram 3.**

Diagram 3

Step 4. Center and sew these longer pieced arcs to the arc/melon units already assembled. See **Diagram 4.** Press all seams toward the melons. Again, refer to page 107 in "Wedding Ring Basics" for more detailed information about sewing curved seams.

Diagram 4

ASSEMBLING THE QUILT TOP

Step 1. Referring to **Diagram 5,** sew the completed arc/melon units to the background A pieces. Be sure to start and stop your seams ¼ inch from each end.

Make 1 for either size.

Make 6 for wallhanging. Make 12 for double.

Make 9 for wallhanging. Make 36 for double.

Diagram 5

Then use a design wall or other flat surface to lay out the units in rows, as shown in the **Partial Assembly Diagram.** The double-size quilt will have seven rows of seven rings each. The wallhanging will have four rows of four rings each.

Step 2. Sew the units together into rows. Sew the rows together to complete the quilt top, as shown in the **Double-Size Quilt Diagram** on page 6. When you sew the units and rows together, you will need to start and stop stitching ¼ inch from each end of the arc. See page 109 for detailed information about assembling the rows.

QUILTING AND FINISHING

Step 1. Mark the quilt top for quilting. In the quilt shown, the rings were outline quilted and have a floral motif in the center.

Step 2. Regardless of which quilt size you have chosen to make, the backing fabric will have to be pieced. **Diagram 6** on page 6 shows the layout for both quilt backs. For the wallhanging, cut the backing fabric in half crosswise, and trim the selvages. Cut one piece in half vertically. Cut a 21-inch-wide panel from the remaining piece. Sew a half-segment to each side of the 21-inch panel.

Step 3. For the double-size quilt, cut the backing fabric crosswise into three equal lengths, and trim the selvages. Cut a 28-inch-wide panel

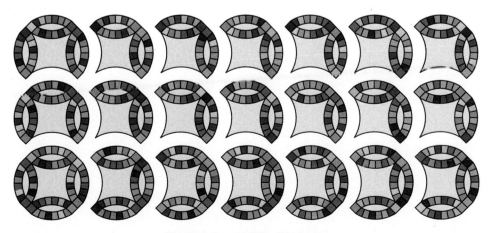

Partial Assembly Diagram

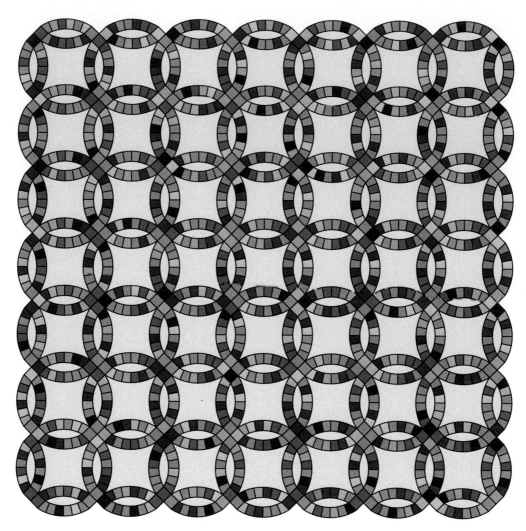

Double-Size Quilt Diagram

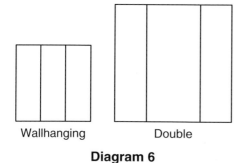

Wallhanging   Double

Diagram 6

from two of the pieces. Sew a 28-inch-wide panel to each side of the full-width panel, as shown. Press the seams open.

Step 4. Layer the backing, batting, and quilt top, and baste. Quilt as desired.

Step 5. Use narrow bias binding to bind the quilt. See page 110 for information about making bias binding and applying it around curves.

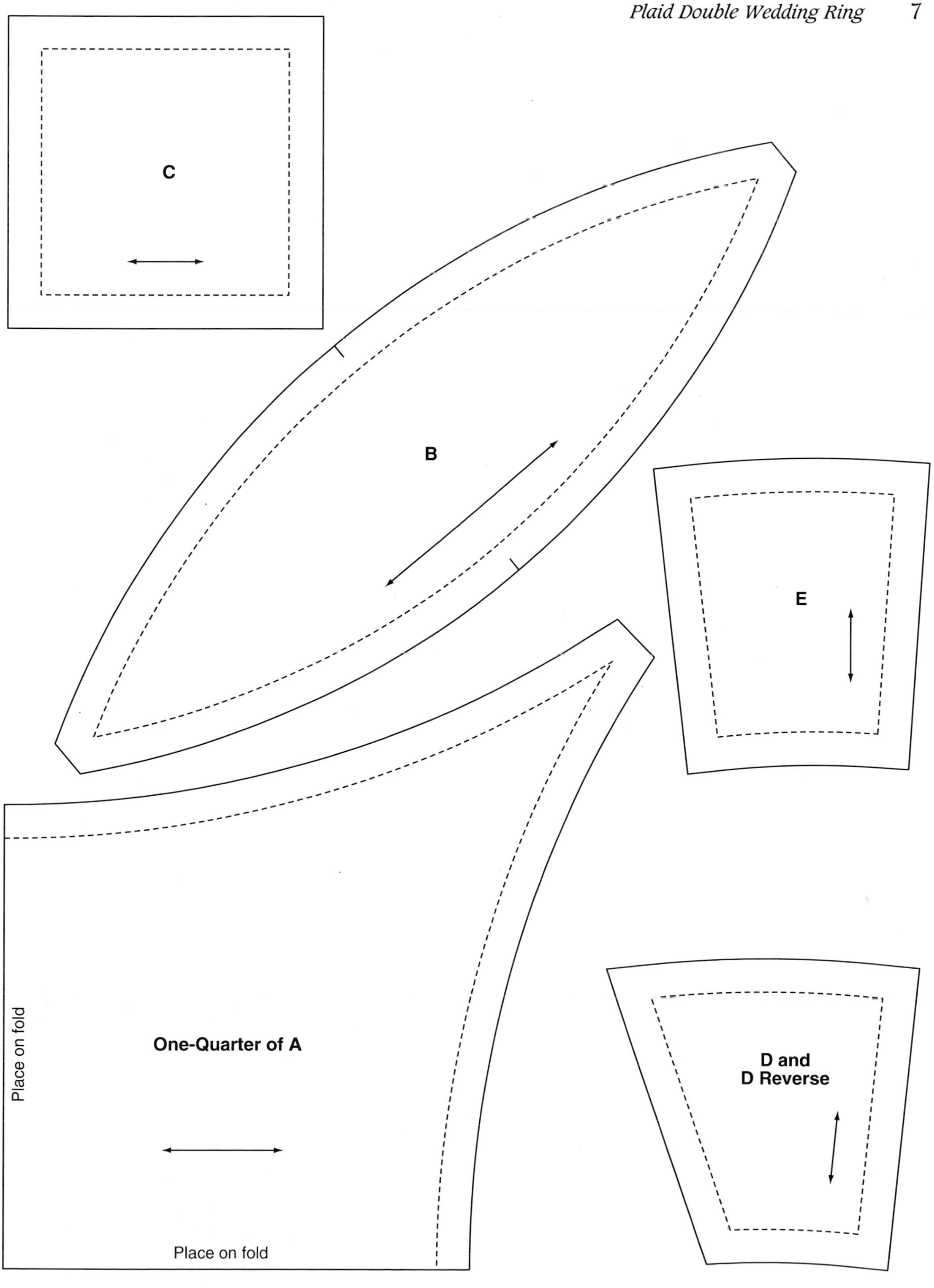

C

B

E

Place on fold

One-Quarter of A

Place on fold

**D and
D Reverse**

DIAMOND WEDDING RING

Skill Level: *Intermediate*

The diamond shapes used in the curved rings of this wallhanging give an exciting new twist to a traditional pattern. Even though the inner diamonds are set in, you'll find the rings in this quilt go together quickly and easily since there are fewer pieces in each arc than in traditional Wedding Rings. Although Joanne Winn named her quilt design for the shape of its pieces, the romantic name of Diamond Wedding Ring makes this a perfect gift for a soon-to-be married couple or for a couple celebrating an important anniversary.

BEFORE YOU BEGIN

This wedding ring quilt features set-in pieces around a diamond shape rather than curves around a traditional melon shape. You may want to refer to page 117 in "Quiltmaking Basics" for more information on setting in pieces.

Diamond Wedding Ring also has a unique border treatment. The rings are assembled into a quilt top, then *appliquéd* onto the four borders, which have been stitched together first. The maker of the quilt shown used invisible machine appliqué to attach her borders; however, you may use the style of appliqué that works best for you. While the skill level for this project is rated intermediate, we recommend that you read through all of the directions before beginning the project to become familiar with the techniques used.

CHOOSING FABRICS

The quilt shown was made with just four fabrics. One of the fabrics used for the rings was repeated in the border, and another fabric was used to bind the quilt. The three colored fabrics are all of similar value (all are medium shades), while the background is light. Darker colors would work together just as well. To help develop your own color scheme for the quilt, photocopy the **Wedding Ring Color Plan** on page 111, and use crayons or colored pencils to experiment with different color arrangements.

Quilt Sizes

	Wallhanging (shown)	Double
Finished Quilt Size	44" × 55¼"	100¼" × 111½"
Finished Ring Diameter	16½"	16½"
Number of Rings	12	72
Number of Pieced Arcs	62	306

Materials

	Wallhanging	Double
Mauve print	1⅝ yards	5¼ yards
Blue-and-mauve print	¾ yard	3¼ yards
Blue solid	½ yard	2 yards
White solid	2 yards	10 yards
Backing	3⅓ yards	9 yards
Batting	50" × 62"	107" × 118"
Binding	½ yard	⅞ yard
Freezer paper (optional)		

NOTE: Yardages are based on 44/45-inch-wide fabrics that are at least 42 inches wide after preshrinking.

Cutting Chart

Fabric	Used For	Piece	Number of Pieces	
			Wallhanging	Double
White	Background	A	12	72
	Diamonds	B	31	153
Mauve print	Rings	C	62	306
Blue-and-mauve print	Rings	C reverse	62	306
Blue	Rings	D	62	306

Fabric	Used For	Strip Width	Number of Strips	
			Wallhanging	Double
Mauve print	Border	6½"	4	10

CUTTING

All measurements include ¼-inch seam allowances. Referring to the Cutting Chart, cut the required number of pieces for your quilt size. Make templates for pieces A, B, C and C reverse, and D using the full-size patterns on pages 14–15. Refer to page 116 in "Quiltmaking Basics" for complete details on making and using templates.

To cut the C and C reverse pieces, lay the mauve print face up on your cutting mat with the blue-and-mauve print face down on top of it. Trace around the C template and cut out both layers at the same time. You will automatically have one mauve print C piece and one blue-and-mauve print C reverse piece. Be sure to follow the grain line arrows on each pattern piece when tracing and cutting.

Note: Cut and piece one sample ring before cutting all of the fabric for the quilt.

PIECING THE RINGS

Step 1. To make a pieced arc, layer a blue-and-mauve print C reverse piece on top of a mauve C piece and stitch along the shortest edge, as shown in **Diagram 1A.** End the seam ¼ inch from the lower edge, as shown, and backstitch. Gently press the seam to one side, taking care not to stretch the unit. See **1B.** Repeat until you've assembled the number of pieced arcs required for your quilt.

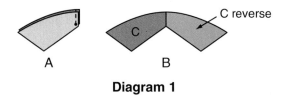

Diagram 1

Step 2. Sew a pieced arc to one side of each white B diamond, as shown in **Diagram 2.** Pivot and continue stitching along the next side of the diamond to set in the piece where you left the seam open when you stitched the C pieces together. For more information on setting in pieces, see page 117 in "Quiltmaking Basics." Press the seam away from the diamond. You will use half of the pieced arcs for this step.

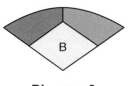

Diagram 2

Since the pieced arcs are identical, you can speed up your piecing by stacking like segments together and positioning the stacks in order near your sewing machine. Or, if you've cut the C and C reverse pieces in layers as discussed in "Cutting," you will already have your pieces layered and ready to go.

Step 3. Sew a blue D diamond to each end of the remaining pieced arcs, as shown in **Diagram 3**. Gently press the seams away from the blue diamonds.

Diagram 3

Step 4. Sew the arcs from Step 3 to the units assembled in Step 2, again pivoting and setting in the white diamonds. Your finished unit will be a pointed oval shape and should look like the one in **Diagram 4**. Press the seam away from the center diamond.

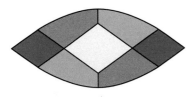

Diagram 4

ASSEMBLING THE QUILT TOP

Step 1. Sew the completed pointed oval units to the white A background pieces, assembling the units in the manner shown in **Diagram 5**.

For the wallhanging, you will have one A piece with a pointed oval sewn to all four sides, five A

pieces with three pointed oval units attached, and six A pieces with only two pointed oval units attached.

For the double-size quilt, you will again have one A piece with pointed ovals attached to all four sides. Fifteen A pieces will have pointed ovals on three sides, and 56 A pieces will have only two pointed ovals attached.

Make 1 for either size.

Make 5 for wallhanging.
Make 15 for double.

Make 6 for wallhanging.
Make 56 for double.

Diagram 5

Step 2. Use a design wall or other flat surface to lay out the units, as shown in the **Wallhanging Assembly Diagram** on page 12. Sew the units together in horizontal rows, starting and stopping each seam 1/4 inch from the ends of the arcs and backstitching.

Refer to page 109 in "Wedding Ring Basics" for more detailed information about assembling the rows of rings.

Step 3. Sew the rows together, again starting and stopping seams 1/4 inch from the end of each arc and backstitching. When completed, the wallhanging will have four horizontal rows of three rings, as shown in the **Wallhanging Diagram** on page 13. The double-size quilt will have nine horizontal rows of eight rings.

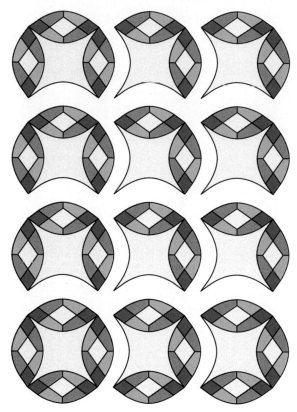

Wallhanging Assembly Diagram

MAKING AND ATTACHING THE BORDERS

For either size quilt, the outside edge of the quilt center is appliquéd onto a preassembled border unit.

Step 1. For the wallhanging, piece together the four 6½-inch-wide mauve print border strips to form one long strip. From this long strip, cut two 44-inch-long strips for the top and bottom borders and two 43¼-inch-long strips for the side borders.

For the double-size quilt, join five 6½-inch-wide mauve print border strips. From this length, cut two 100¼-inch-long strips for the top and bottom borders. Join five more mauve print strips, and cut the completed long strip into two 99½-inch-long strips for the side borders.

Step 2. For either size quilt, sew a side border to a top or bottom border, placing the right sides

together and aligning the outer edges, as shown in **Diagram 6A.** Press the seams toward the side borders, as shown in **6B.** Repeat, sewing and pressing all corners to assemble the entire border unit, as shown in **6C.**

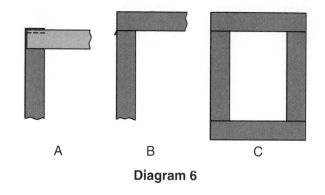

Diagram 6

Step 3. Prepare the outer rings for appliqué. Refer to page 109 in "Wedding Ring Basics" for details about the freezer paper method of preparing the ring edges for appliqué. Or use your favorite method of appliqué. Center the completed quilt top on the border. Pin or baste it in place, then hand or machine appliqué the top to the border around the outer rings. The **Wallhanging Diagram** shows how the completed wallhanging will look. The double-size quilt is finished in the same manner—it simply has more rings to appliqué.

Step 4. Trim any excess fabric from the inner portion of the border as necessary to eliminate excess bulk. If you appliquéd using the freezer paper method, remove the paper now.

QUILTING AND FINISHING

Step 1. Mark the quilt top for quilting, if desired. The quilt shown has machine stipple quilting in the print areas of the pieced arcs and in a portion of the border. A floral and leaf quilting stencil was used to mark the remainder of the quilt.

Step 2. Regardless of which quilt size you've chosen to make, the backing will have to be pieced.

Wallhanging Diagram

For the wallhanging, cut the backing fabric into two equal lengths, and trim the selvages. Cut a 32-inch-wide panel from one length and a 16-inch-wide panel from the remaining length. Sew the two panels together, as shown in **Diagram 7**. Press the seams open.

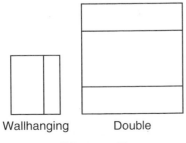

Wallhanging   Double

Diagram 7

Step 3. For the double-size quilt, cut the backing fabric into three equal lengths, and trim the selvages. Cut a 33½-inch-wide panel from two of the segments, then sew one of these to each side of the remaining full-width piece, as shown. Press the seams open.

Step 4. Layer the backing, batting, and quilt top, and baste. Quilt as desired.

Step 5. Referring to the directions on page 121 in "Quiltmaking Basics," make and attach double-fold binding. To calculate the approximate number of inches of binding needed for the quilt size you are making, add the length of the four sides of the quilt plus 9 inches.

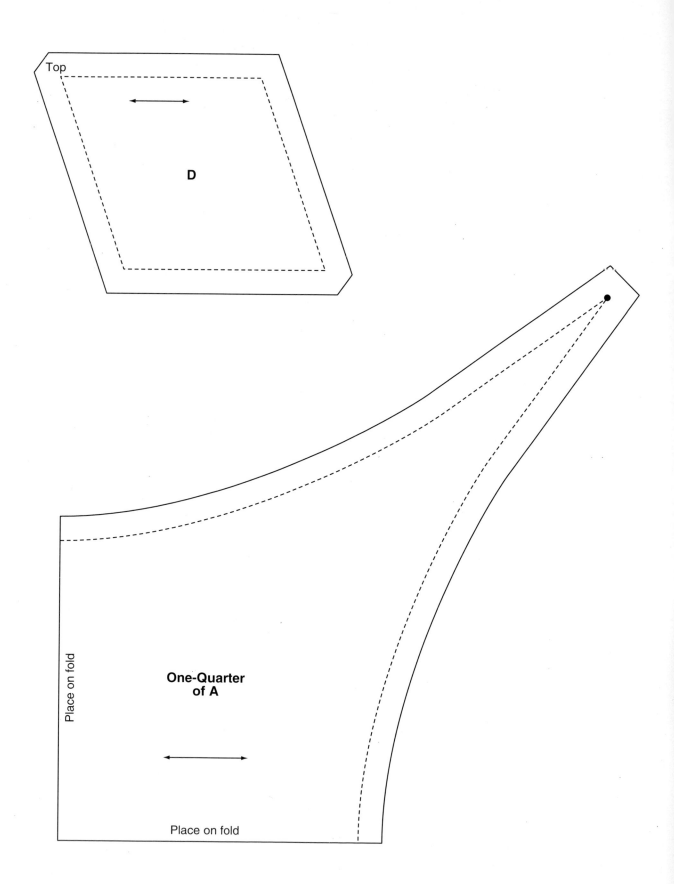

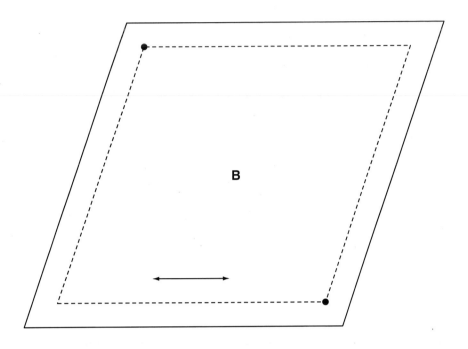

B

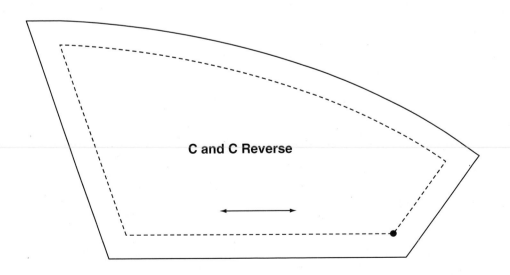

C and C Reverse

Is This Wedded Bliss?

Skill Level: *Intermediate*

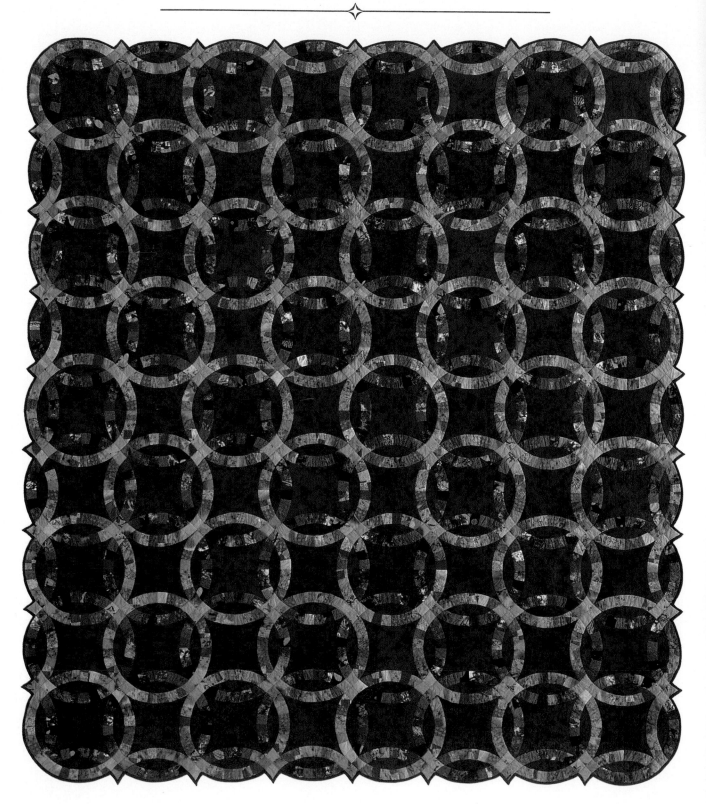

M aureen Carlson of Illinois created this regal double-size Wedding Ring quilt. The quilt's full name, "Is This Wedded Bliss, or Have I Dyed and Gone to Heaven?" says it all. It is heavenly, and the lush purple fabric Maureen hand dyed is a big part of the quilt's appeal. What better fabrics to contrast with the velvety texture of hand-dyed cotton than splashy, tropical batiks!

BEFORE YOU BEGIN

If this is your first Double Wedding Ring quilt, be sure to read "Wedding Ring Basics," beginning on page 104, before starting the project. Although each project in this book contains specific information unique to its assembly, many aspects of construction are similar from quilt to quilt.

You will need to make templates for pattern pieces A, B, C, D, and E on page 21. For information on making and using templates, see page 116 in "Quiltmaking Basics."

CHOOSING FABRICS

The quiltmaker hand dyed her own fabric for the background and melons in this quilt. If you like the hand-dyed look but don't want to do it yourself, check your local quilt shop, which may carry hand-dyed fabrics. You could also choose a solid fabric for the background. The rings were pieced from an assortment of purchased batik fabrics in shades varying from pink to rose to wine, with occasional vibrant blues, oranges, greens, and blue-greens added for visual appeal. Batiked fabrics are readily available, so you can choose from a variety of colors and designs.

To develop your own color scheme for the quilt, photocopy the **Wedding Ring Color Plan** on page 111, and use crayons or colored pencils to experiment with different color arrangements.

CUTTING

All measurements include ¼-inch seam allowances. Referring

Quilt Sizes

	Wallhanging	Double (shown)
Finished Quilt Size	33½" × 33½"	81" × 90½"
Finished Ring Diameter	15"	15"
Number of Rings	12	72
Number of Pieced Arcs	62	322

Materials

	Wallhanging	Double (shown)
Purple hand-dyed solid	1⅜ yards	7½ yards
Assorted batiks	1⅝ yards	7⅔ yards
Pink batik	¼ yard	¾ yard
Green batik	¼ yard	¾ yard
Backing	1¼ yards	7⅝ yards
Batting	42" × 42"	89" × 99"
Binding	¾ yard	1 yard

NOTE: Yardages are based on 44/45-inch-wide fabrics that are at least 42 inches wide after preshrinking. Be sure to check the width of hand-dyed fabrics before purchasing them because sometimes they are sold in narrower widths. Adjust your yardages if necessary.

17

Cutting Chart

Fabric	Used For	Piece	Number of Pieces	
			Wallhanging	Double
Purple	Background	A	12	72
	Melons	B	31	161
Pink batik	Connecting wedges	C	36	176
Green batik	Connecting wedges	C	36	176
Assorted batiks	Outer wedges of arcs	D	62	322
	Outer wedges of arcs	D reverse	62	322
	Inner wedges of arcs	E	248	1,288

to the Cutting Chart, cut the required number of pieces for your quilt size.

Note: Cut and piece one sample ring before cutting all of the fabric for the quilt.

PIECING THE ARCS

Step 1. Stack the D, D reverse, and E pieces in separate piles. Begin each pieced arc with a D piece. To the right of it, sew a succession of four E pieces. End the arc with a D reverse piece. As you sew, be sure the pieces are oriented so that curves arch in the same direction, as shown in **Diagram 1**. Gently press all seams in the same direction, taking care not to stretch the unit. Repeat until you've assembled all arcs required for your quilt.

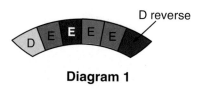

Diagram 1

Step 2. Center and sew a pieced arc to one side of each purple B melon, as shown in **Diagram 2**. Refer to page 107 in "Wedding Ring Basics" for specific information and tips on assembling the curved pieces common to most Double Wedding Ring quilts. Press seams toward the melons. You will use half of the pieced arcs for this step.

Diagram 2

Step 3. Sew a green batik C piece to each D end of the remaining arcs, as shown in **Diagram 3**. Sew a pink batik C piece to each D reverse end of the arcs, as shown. Gently press the seams in the same direction as other seams in the arc.

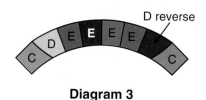

Diagram 3

—— Sew Easy ——

Make sure you mix up your assortment of fabrics for a pleasing overall use of color. For example, if you have selected a few hot colors, as in the quilt shown, use them randomly and sparingly for a hit of electric blue here and a spot of tangerine there.

Step 4. Center and sew these longer pieced arcs to the arc/melon units you already assembled, as shown in **Diagram 4.** Press all seams toward the melons. Again, refer to page 107 in "Wedding Ring Basics" for further help with sewing curved seams.

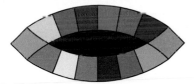

Diagram 4

ASSEMBLING THE QUILT TOP

Step 1. Use a design wall or other flat surface to lay out the completed arc/melon units and the A background pieces in rows, as shown in the **Partial Assembly Diagram.** Note that the orientation of arc/melon units changes from row to row, so refer to the diagram or the photograph on page 16 for directional placement of the pink and green tips of the arc/melon units. For the double-size quilt, you will have nine horizontal rows of eight rings each. For the wallhanging, you will have four horizontal rows of three rings each. The C pieces shown will be added after the rows are assembled.

Step 2. Sew the units into horizontal rows. You will need to start and stop stitching ¼ inch from

each end of the arcs as you attach them to the purple background pieces. Refer to page 109 in "Wedding Ring Basics" for more information on sewing curved pieces into rows.

Step 3. Sew the rows together, starting and stopping your seams ¼ inch from the end of each arc, to complete the quilt top.

Step 4. After the quilt top is assembled, set in the remaining C pieces where the arcs intersect around the perimeter of the quilt, referring to the **Partial Assembly Diagram.** Be sure that the square corner of all of the C pieces points in toward the quilt. Notice that the colors alternate from row to row.

QUILTING AND FINISHING

Step 1. Mark the quilt top for quilting. The quilt shown was hand quilted with a floral motif in the center of each ring. It was also quilted in the ditch around each ring.

Step 2. The backing for the wallhanging is made from a single panel of 42-inch-wide fabric. Trim the selvages and press the 1¼-yard length of backing fabric.

Step 3. For the double-size quilt, cut the backing fabric into three equal lengths, and trim the selvages. Cut a 29-inch-wide panel from two of the lengths, then sew one panel to each side of

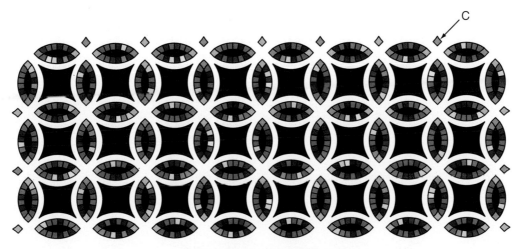

Partial Assembly Diagram

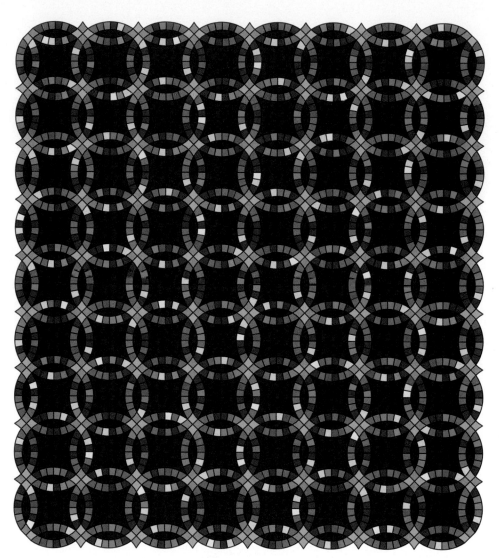

Double-Size Quilt Diagram

the full-width panel, as shown in **Diagram 5.**
Press the seams open.

Step 4. Layer the backing, batting, and quilt
top, and baste. Quilt as desired.

Step 5. Use narrow bias binding to bind the
quilt. See page 110 for details on making bias
binding and applying it around curves.

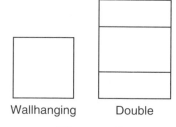

Wallhanging   Double

Diagram 5

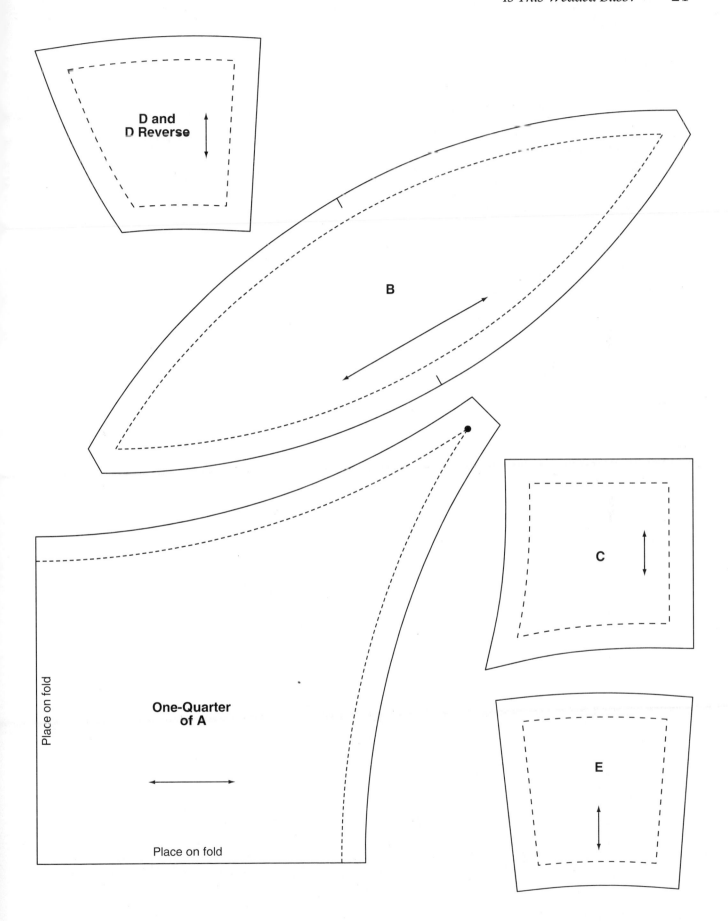

D and
D Reverse

B

C

One-Quarter
of A

Place on fold

Place on fold

E

JOB'S TEARS

Skill Level: *Intermediate*

*Q*uiltmakers and teachers Susan Bushnell and Suzzy Payne made this Job's Tears quilt when they were researching quilt patterns with a biblical reference for their book Creative American Quilting Inspired by the Bible. While the pattern is not technically a Double Wedding Ring, it is closely related. This quilt pattern is also known by other names, among them Slave Chain, Texas Tears, and Rocky Road to Kansas. Job's Tears requires sewing curves and setting in seams as do most of the other quilts in this book. However, you may find it a bit easier to construct since you can use standard straight line assembly, rather than continuing with more curved sewing, once the blocks are made.

BEFORE YOU BEGIN

Each 16-inch Job's Tears block is composed of four 8-inch quarter blocks. Each of these quarter blocks is assembled in the same way. Then four quarter-blocks are positioned to form a complete block, as shown in the **Block Diagram** on page 24.

You will need to make templates from pattern pieces A, B, C, D, E, F, and G on pages 28–31. For information on making and using templates, see page 116.

CHOOSING FABRICS

The C pentagons are all from the same small-scale dark blue print. Since four pentagons meet to form links for the rings, their uniformity ties the rings together. Select the fabric for these pieces carefully, since the octagon formed when the C pieces are joined together is fairly large. You want neither a fabric that will overpower your quilt nor one that

Quilt Sizes

	Double (shown)	King
Finished Quilt Size	82½" × 98½"	114½" × 114½"
Finished Block Size	16"	16"
Number of Blocks	20	36

Materials

	Double	King
Muslin	7¾ yards	12¾ yards
Dark blue print	¾ yard	1½ yards
Assorted prints	3½ yards	5¾ yards
Blue print	¾ yard	1⅛ yards
Rose print	½ yard	⅝ yard
Backing	7¾ yards	10 yards
Batting	90" × 106"	120" × 120"
Binding	¾ yard	1 yard

NOTE: Yardages are based on 44/45-inch-wide fabrics that are at least 42 inches wide after preshrinking.

will fade into the background.

The curved A strips are cut from assorted medium- to dark-value prints of varying colors. The yardage requirement for these strips is estimated. For a scrappy quilt such as this, you will likely begin with more actual yardage but have leftover pieces for your next scrap project. The

Cutting Chart

Fabric	Used For	Piece	Number of Pieces	
			Double	King
Muslin	Melons	B	80	144
	Background crescents	D	160	288
	Middle border	5" strips	7	10
Dark blue print	Pentagons	C	160	288
Assorted prints	Curved strips	A	160	288
	Center fan blades	E	4	4
	Inner fan blades	F	4	4
	Inner fan blades	F reverse	4	4
	Outer fan blades	G	4	4
	Outer fan blades	G reverse	4	4
Blue print	Outer border	3½" strips	7	10
Rose print	Inner border	2" strips	7	10

fan blades in the corners are assembled from the same assortment of prints used in the curved strips.

To develop your own color scheme for the quilt, photocopy the **Wedding Ring Color Plan** on page 111, and use crayons or colored pencils to experiment with different color arrangements.

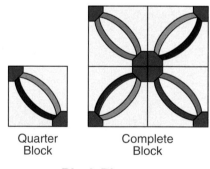

Quarter Block   Complete Block

Block Diagram

CUTTING

All measurements include ¼-inch seam allowances. Referring to the Cutting Chart, cut the required number of pieces for your quilt size.

Note: Cut and piece one sample block before cutting all of the fabric for the quilt.

PIECING THE BLOCKS

Step 1. With right sides together, pin a curved A strip to a B melon, matching centers. Sew the pieces together with the curved strip on top, as shown in **Diagram 1**. Ease the strip's edge to fit the melon. Press the seam toward the strip.

Step 2. In the same manner, sew a curved strip to the opposite side of the melon, as shown in **Diagram 2**, and press the seam toward the strip.

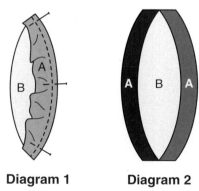

Diagram 1   **Diagram 2**

Step 3. With right sides together, align a C pentagon with one end of a melon unit, matching the straight edges. The point of the melon unit will extend slightly beyond the aligned edge. With the melon unit on top, sew the pieces together, beginning and ending your seam ¼ inch from either side of the melon unit's outer edges. Your seam should cross the intersection where the curved pieces were sewn to the melon, as shown in **Diagram 3A.** Repeat on the opposite end of the melon. Press the seams toward the pentagons to complete the melon/pentagon unit, as shown in **3B.**

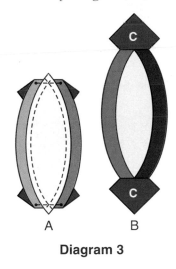

Diagram 3

Step 4. To attach a D crescent piece to the melon/pentagon unit, match a short side of the pentagon to the narrow end of a crescent and pin the pieces. Referring to **Diagram 4,** set in seam 1. Begin stitching ¼ inch from the inside corner and stitch to the end of the pieces, as indicated by the directional arrow. For details on setting in seams, see page 117.

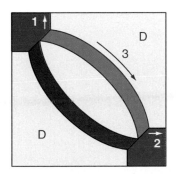

Diagram 4

Step 5. Match the pentagon at the opposite end of the melon unit with the opposite narrow end of

the crescent, as shown, and pin the seams together. Sew seam 2 following the direction of the arrow, beginning the seam ¼ inch from the inside corner of the pentagon.

Step 6. With the crescent piece on top, sew the crescent to the melon unit along the curved strip, easing in seam 3 to fit. Sew in the direction of the arrow, starting and stopping stitching ¼ inch from each end of the crescent.

Step 7. Add a second D crescent to the opposite side of the melon unit in the same manner, completing a quarter block. Press all seams.

Step 8. Repeat Steps 1 through 7 to make three more quarter blocks. Lay out four quarter blocks, as shown in the **Block Diagram,** and sew them together, matching pentagon seams carefully.

Step 9. Repeat, making the number of complete blocks required for your quilt size.

ASSEMBLING THE QUILT TOP

Step 1. Using a design wall or other flat surface, lay out the blocks in rows, as shown in the **Double-Size Assembly Diagram** on page 26, until you are pleased with the color arrangement. As shown, the double size has five vertical rows of four blocks each. For the king-size quilt, you will have six vertical rows of six blocks each. Press seams in adjoining rows in opposite directions.

Step 2. Sew the rows together, matching seams carefully. Press all seams.

ATTACHING THE BORDERS

Three borders are used in this quilt, with a large pieced fan radiating outward from each corner.

Step 1. Sew an F and F reverse piece to either side of the E center piece, as shown in **Diagram 5** on page 26. Then sew a G piece to the F piece and a G reverse piece to the F reverse piece, as shown. Press all seams in one direction. Repeat, making three more fan units.

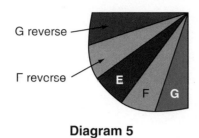

G reverse
F reverse

E
F
G

Diagram 5

Double-Size Assembly Diagram

Step 2. The border strips for each side of the quilt are sewn together, then added to the quilt as a single unit. To make the top and bottom borders, measure the width of the quilt top, taking the measurement through the horizontal center of the quilt rather than along the edge. Piece the rose border strips end to end, then from the long border strip, cut two strips to the measured length. Repeat with the muslin and blue strips.

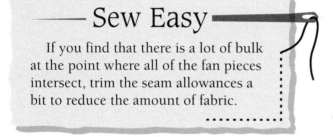

— Sew Easy

If you find that there is a lot of bulk at the point where all of the fan pieces intersect, trim the seam allowances a bit to reduce the amount of fabric.

Step 3. Pin and sew an outer blue border strip to a muslin border strip. Pin and sew a rose inner border strip to the opposite side of the muslin strip, referring to **Diagram 6**. Press the seams toward the dark borders. Repeat with remaining three strips to make the border for the other end of the quilt.

Diagram 6

Step 4. To make the side borders, measure the length of the quilt top, taking the measurement through the vertical center of the quilt rather than

along the sides. Piece like-color strips together to achieve two strips of the necessary length as you did for the top and bottom borders.

Step 5. Sew the strips together into two border units as you did with top and bottom borders. See **Diagram 6**.

Step 6. Sew a completed fan to each end of the side borders, as shown in **Diagram 7**.

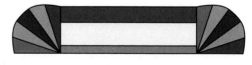

Diagram 7

Step 7. Fold the completed top border in half crosswise and crease. Unfold it and position it right side down along the top edge of the quilt, with the crease at the vertical midpoint. Pin at the midpoint and ends first, then along the length of

Double-Size Quilt Diagram

the entire end, easing in fullness if necessary. Sew the border to the quilt top using a ¹⁄₄-inch seam allowance. Press the seam toward the border. Repeat on the opposite end of the quilt.

Step 8. Fold a completed side border unit in half crosswise and crease. Unfold it and position it right side down along one side of the quilt, with the crease at the horizontal midpoint. Pin at the midpoint and ends first, then along the length of the entire side, easing in fullness if necessary and matching seams where the fan edge meets the inner rose border at the top and bottom of the quilt. Sew the border to the quilt using a ¹⁄₄-inch seam allowance. Press the seam toward the border.

Repeat on the opposite side of the quilt. See the **Double-Size Quilt Diagram.**

QUILTING AND FINISHING

Step 1. Mark the quilt top for quilting. The quilt shown has a combination of cross-hatching and outline quilting. Teardrops were quilted in the borders and the muslin crescents.

Step 2. Regardless of which quilt size you've chosen to make, the backing will have to be pieced. To make the backing for the double-size quilt, cut the backing fabric crosswise into three

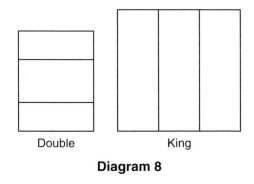

Sew Easy

To quickly and easily mark quilting lines, try a hera. Sold in most quilt shops, this plastic tool fits in the palm of your hand. By pressing the curved edge along the fabric, you create an indentation in the fabric that serves as a quilting guide. Once you're done stitching, there are no lines to erase!

Diagram 8

equal lengths, and trim the selvages. Cut a 33-inch-wide panel from two of the pieces, then sew one of these to each side of the full-width piece, as shown in **Diagram 8.** For the king-size quilt, cut the backing fabric crosswise into three equal lengths, and trim the selvages. Sew the three panels together lengthwise, as shown. Press the seams open.

Step 3. Layer the backing, batting, and quilt top, and baste. Quilt as desired.

Step 4. Make and attach double-fold binding, referring to the directions on page 121 in "Quiltmaking Basics" for more information. To calculate the amount of binding needed for your quilt size, add the length of the four sides of the quilt plus 9 inches. The total is the approximate number of inches of binding you will need.

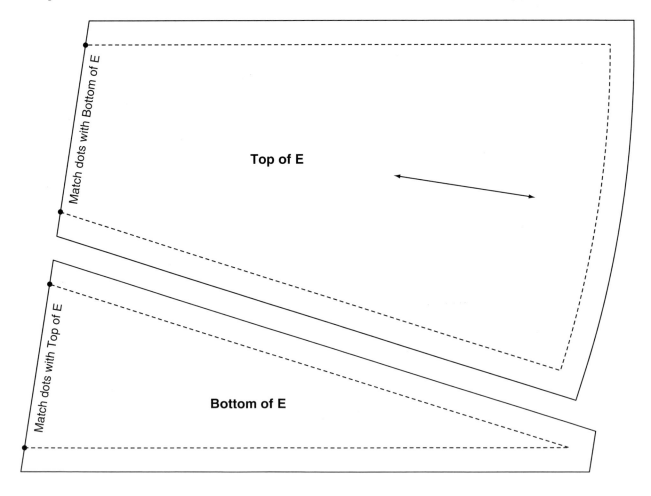

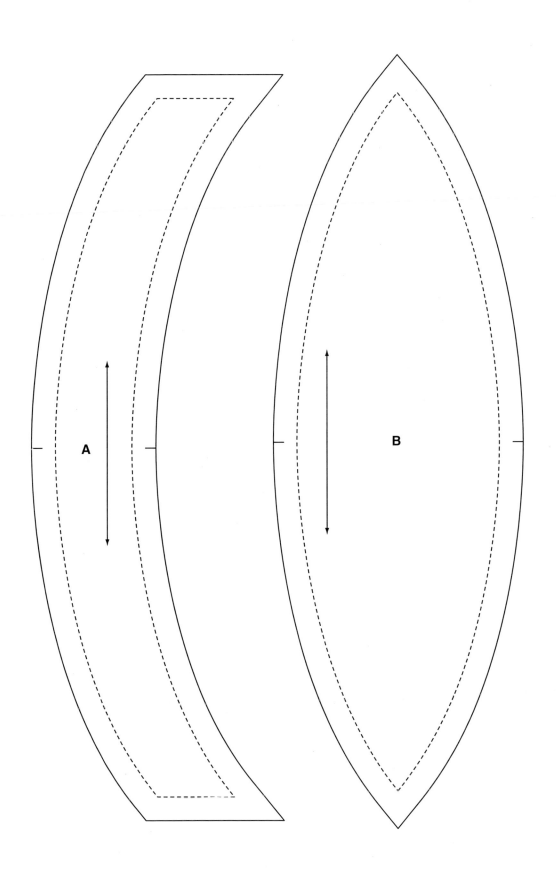

A

B

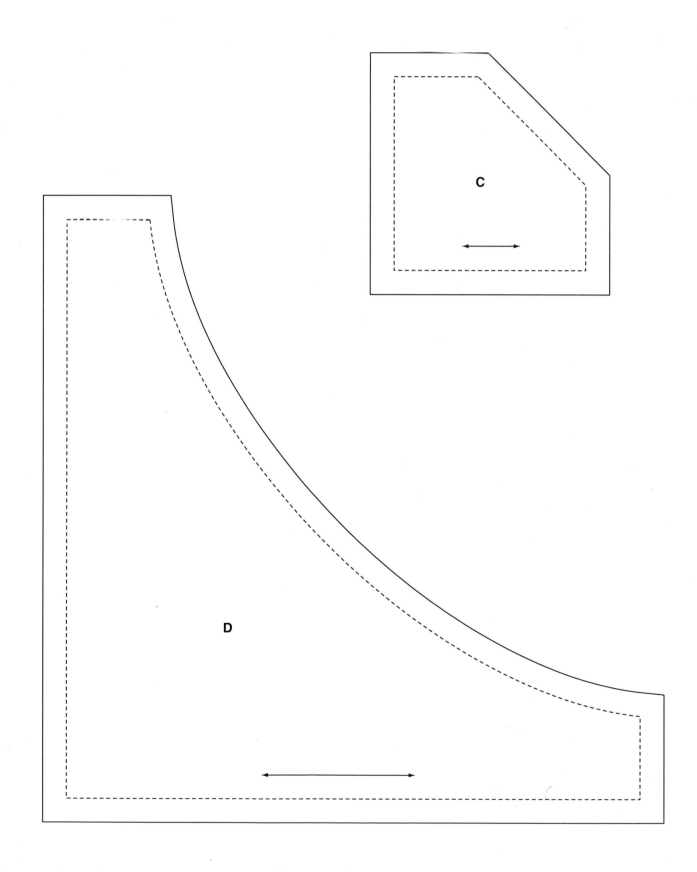

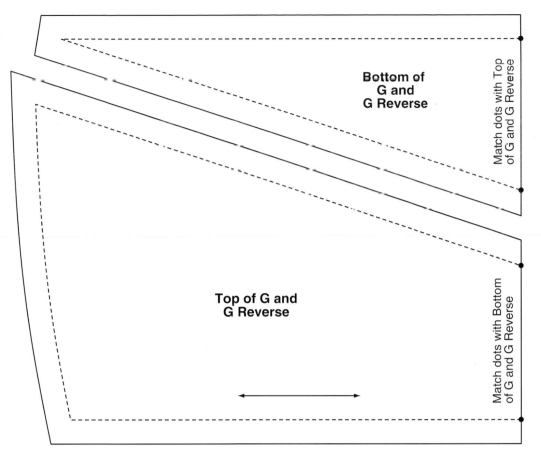

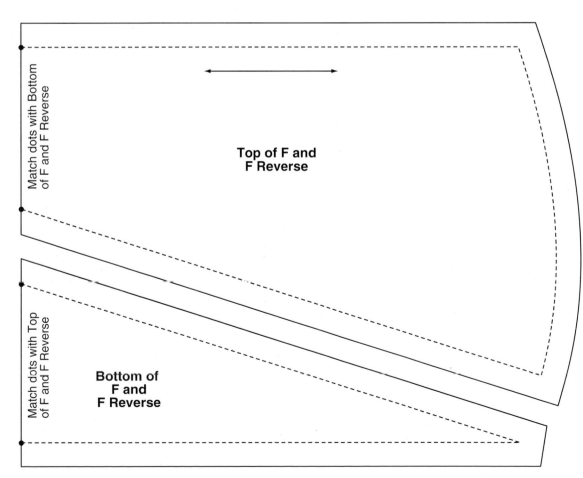

Hearts and Hands

Skill Level: *Advanced*

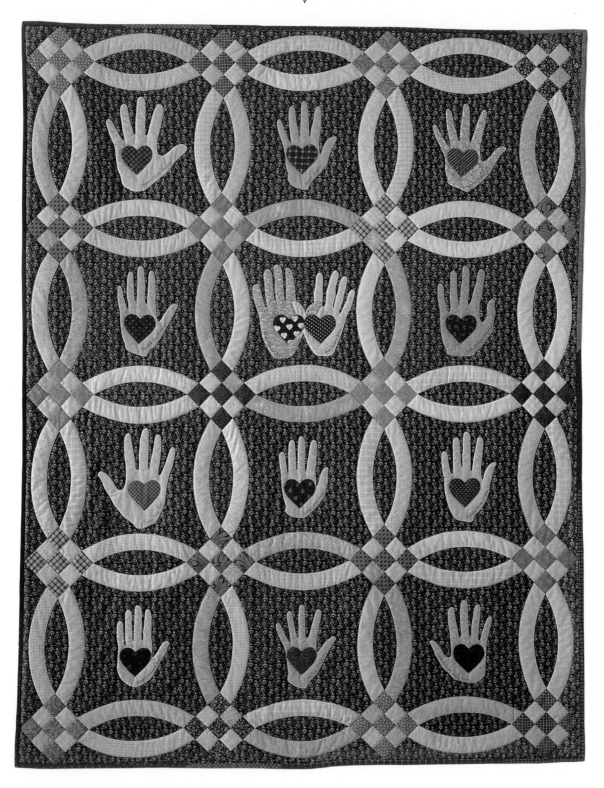

*H*earts and hands are familiar folk art motifs, yet they are an unusual addition to a Double Wedding Ring. Quiltmaker Debbie Timby designed this original lap quilt as a golden wedding anniversary gift for her parents, thus the yellow and gold rings. Each hand is unique—they are traced from and signed by family members. The Nine-Patch connecting blocks between the rings add to the country charm of this quilt, but they were really planned as a way to push the rings far enough apart to allow the hands to fit comfortably inside. In addition to being a wonderful family keepsake, this quilt would make a charming friendship project.

Before You Begin

If this is your first Double Wedding Ring quilt, be sure to read "Wedding Ring Basics," beginning on page 104, before starting the project. Although each project in this book contains specific information for its own assembly, there are similarities in assembly techniques.

You will need to make templates for the Wedding Ring pieces as well as for the heart and hand. Patterns for pieces A, B, C, D, and E are on pages 38–39. The center point marks on the curved pattern pieces will help you set in seams more easily. You will need to trace your own hand or one from a family member or friend to make a hand template. For more information on making and using templates, see page 116 in "Quiltmaking Basics."

Choosing Fabrics

The background pieces in this quilt were all sewn from the same dark brown calico print. In

keeping with the folk art feel, any country-flavored calico would work well, as long as it contrasts with the fabrics selected for the rings. For her rings, the quilt-

maker chose a variety of yellow print fabrics, which are repeated again in the Nine-Patch blocks. She also used several different medium and dark blue prints

Quilt Sizes

	Lap (shown)	Queen
Finished Quilt Size	48½" × 62½"	96" × 96"
Finished Ring Diameter	19"	19"
Number of Rings	12	36
Number of Nine-Patch Blocks	20	49

Materials

	Lap	Queen
Assorted yellow prints	2½ yards	7⅛ yards
Assorted blue prints	⅜ yard	1 yard
Assorted red prints	⅜ yard	⅞ yard
Assorted beige prints	⅞ yard	3 yards
Dark brown print	3 yards	8¾ yards
Backing	1⅞ yards	9⅝ yards
Batting	57" × 71"	104" × 104"
Binding	½ yard	¾ yard

Note: Yardages are based on 44/45-inch-wide fabrics that are at least 42 inches wide after preshrinking.

33

Cutting Chart

Fabric	Used For	Piece	Number of Pieces	
			Lap	Queen
Dark brown print	Background	A	12	36
	Melons	B	31	84
	Outer background	C	14	24
	Quilt corners	4⅛" square	2	2
Yellow prints	Arcs	D	62	168
Red prints	Hearts	E	12	36
Beige prints	Hands		13	37

Fabric	Used For	Strip Width	Number of Strips	
			Lap	Queen
Blue prints	Nine-Patch blocks	2"	5	16
Yellow prints	Nine-Patch blocks	2"	4	13

along with the yellows in the Nine-Patch blocks. You can cut each strip from a different fabric or cut them all from the same blue fabric. Or substitute shades of country reds or greens.

The hands are cut from an assortment of beige prints, and red hearts are appliquéd to the hands. Red is used again in the scrappy binding.

CUTTING

All measurements include ¼-inch seam allowances. Referring to the Cutting Chart, cut the required number of pieces for your quilt size. The rings of this quilt are constructed using templates, but the Nine-Patch blocks connecting the rings are assembled using strip-piecing techniques.

Note: Cut and piece one sample ring and Nine-Patch block before cutting all the fabric for the quilt.

PIECING THE ARC/MELON UNITS

Step 1. Pin a D arc to a B melon, matching centers. Stitch the pieces together, as shown in **Diagram 1A.** Do not stitch into the seam al-

lowance; begin and end the seam ¼ inch from each end of the arc. Press the seam toward the arc.

Step 2. In the same manner, center and sew a second yellow arc to the opposite side of the melon, as shown in **1B.** Gently press the seam toward the arc. For a scrappy look, sew a different yellow fabric to each side of the melon.

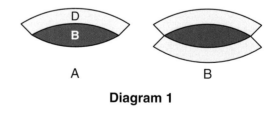

Diagram 1

Step 3. Repeat Steps 1 and 2 to assemble all of the arc/melon units required for your quilt.

PIECING THE NINE-PATCH BLOCKS

Each Nine-Patch block is made from segments of two different strip sets, as shown in **Diagram 2.** The directions are for using short strip sets to yield a scrappy look. If you prefer, you can use 42-inch strips to yield more blocks from each strip.

Diagram 2

Step 1. Select one blue strip and two different yellow strips. From the blue strip, cut two 16½-inch-long pieces and one 8¼-inch-long piece. From the yellow strips, cut one 16½-inch-long piece and two 8¼-inch-long pieces. Set aside the leftover pieces of the strips.

Step 2. To make Strip Set 1, sew a 16½-inch blue strip to each side of the long yellow strip, as shown in **Diagram 3**. Press seams toward the blue strips. Using a rotary cutter and ruler, square up one end of the strip set. Cut eight 2-inch-wide segments from the strip set, as shown.

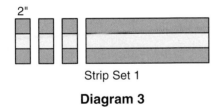

Strip Set 1

Diagram 3

Step 3. To make Strip Set 2, sew the short yellow strips to each side of the short blue strip, as shown in **Diagram 4**. Press the seams toward the blue strip. Cut the strip set into four 2-inch-wide segments.

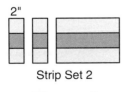

Strip Set 2

Diagram 4

Step 4. Sew two Strip Set 1 segments and one Strip Set 2 segment together, as shown in **Diagram 5**, matching seams carefully. Repeat with the remaining segments.

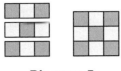

Diagram 5

Step 5. Repeat Steps 1 through 4 to complete the Nine-Patch blocks required for your quilt.

ASSEMBLING THE QUILT TOP

Step 1. Sew each outer background C piece to one side of an arc/melon unit, as shown in **Diagram 6**, starting and stopping ¼ inch from the end of each arc. Press seams toward the C pieces.

Diagram 6

Step 2. Use a design wall or other flat surface to lay out arc/melon units and background A pieces, as shown in the **Partial Assembly Diagram**.

Partial Assembly Diagram

Step 3. Sew the units together, beginning at the upper left corner and working across and down. Do not stitch into the seam allowances. If you are making the lap quilt, your quilt top should look like **Diagram 7**. For the queen-size quilt, your quilt top will have six rows of six rings each.

Diagram 7

Step 4. Pin a Nine-Patch block in each "hole" between the rings, with right sides together. Sew one side of a Nine-Patch block to the quilt, matching the seams with the seam intersections of the arcs and A pieces in the quilt. Start and stop sewing ¼ inch from the ends of the block, as indicated by the dots in **Diagram 8A**. Remove the quilt from your sewing machine and stitch the next side of the block. Repeat until all sides of all blocks are sewn to the rings. See **8B**. Press the quilt top.

Stitch from dot to dot
A

Completed set-in Nine Patch
B

Diagram 8

Step 5. Cut the 4⅛-inch dark brown squares in half diagonally, as shown in **Diagram 9**. Center and sew a triangle to each corner of the quilt.

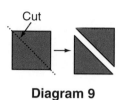
Cut

Diagram 9

Appliquéing the Hearts and Hands

Step 1. Prepare the number of hearts and hands needed for your quilt size for appliqué. Refer to page 118 in "Quiltmaking Basics" for information about needle-turn appliqué, or use the appliqué method of your choice.

Step 2. Appliqué the hands to the rings as desired. Referring to the **Lap Quilt Diagram** or the photograph on page 32, you'll notice that the hands on the quilt shown do not all face the same direction. Also notice that the quiltmaker appliquéd two interlocking hands in one of the center rings. Appliqué a red heart on top of each hand. Use a permanent marking pen to write the person's name, date of birth, or other personal information on each hand or heart, if desired.

Quilting and Finishing

Step 1. Mark the quilt top for quilting. Outline quilting was used to highlight the rings, hearts, and hands in the original quilt. Cross-hatching or stipple quilting could be done in the rings to make the hands stand out.

Step 2. Regardless of which quilt size you have chosen to make, the backing will have to be pieced. For the lap quilt, cut the backing fabric in half crosswise, and trim the selvages. Cut two 15-inch-wide panels from the entire length of one piece. Sew a narrow panel to each side of the full-width piece, as shown in **Diagram 10**.

Lap Quilt Diagram

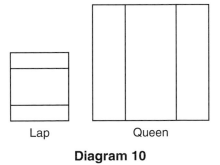

Lap   Queen

Diagram 10

Step 3. For the queen-size quilt, cut the backing fabric into three equal lengths, and trim the selvages. Cut a 36-inch wide panel from two of the pieces. Sew a 36-inch panel to each side of the full-width panel, as shown in the diagram. Press the seams open.

Step 4. Layer the backing, batting, and quilt top, and baste. Quilt as desired.

Step 5. Referring to page 121 in "Quiltmaking Basics," make and attach double-fold binding. To calculate the amount of binding needed for your quilt size, add the length of the four sides of the quilt plus 9 inches. The total is the approximate number of inches of binding you will need.

The quilt shown is framed in a scrappy red binding. Short lengths of the same print fabrics used for the hearts were sewn end to end to make the binding.

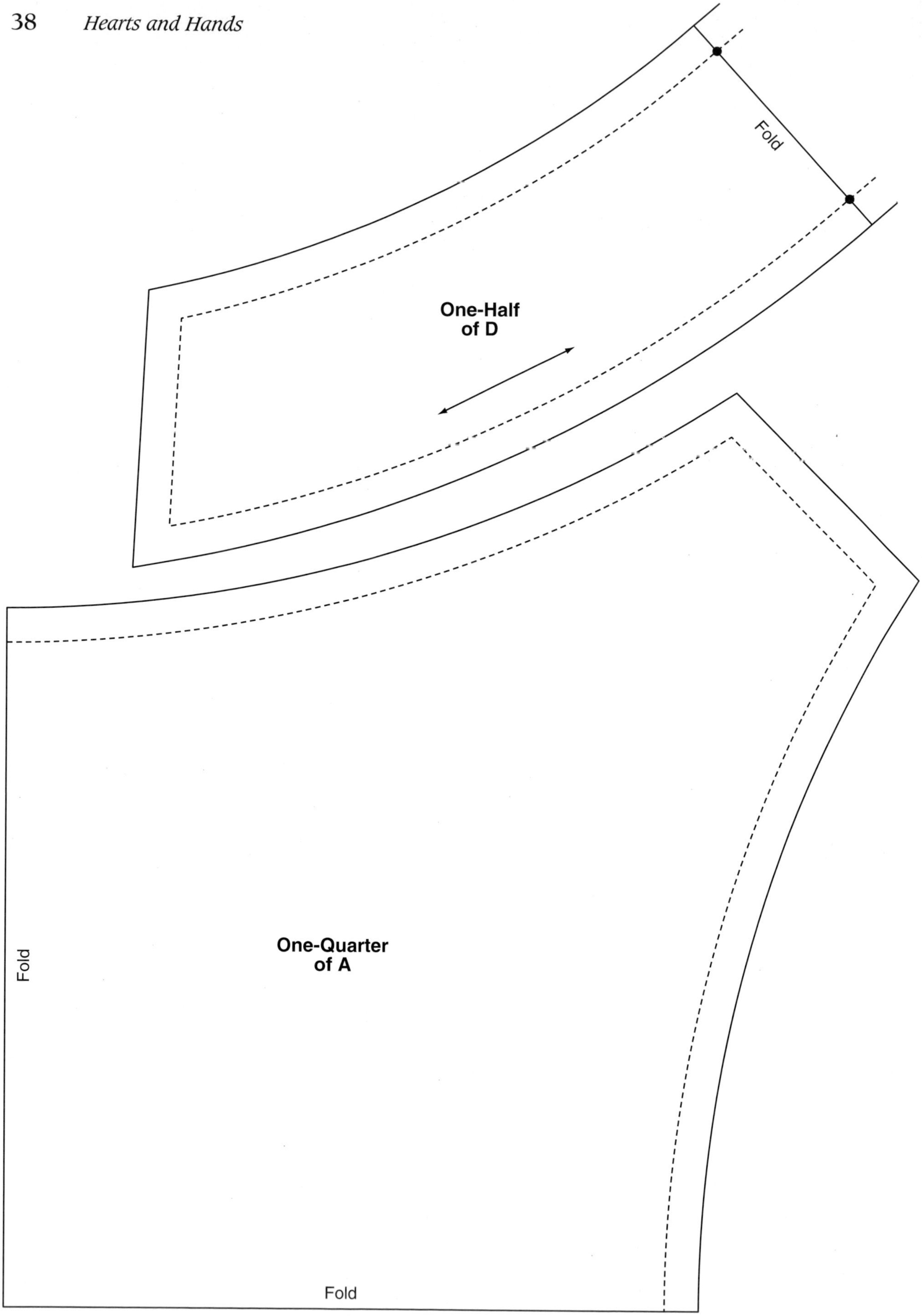

**One-Half
of D**

Fold

**One-Quarter
of A**

Fold

Fold

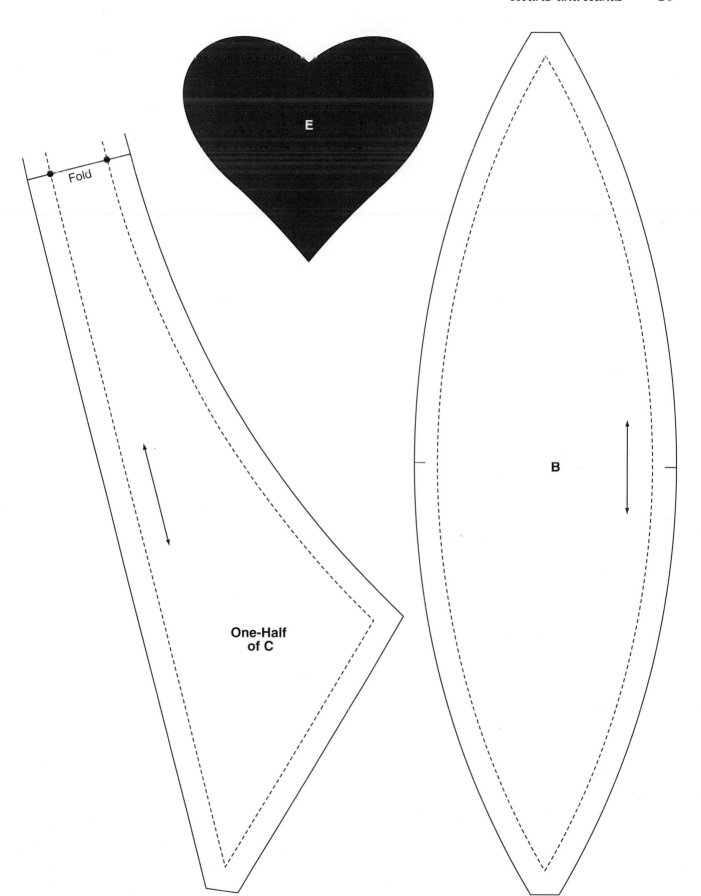

E

Fold

One-Half
of C

B

ROSE RINGS

Skill Level: *Challenging*

Quiltmaker Susan Stein combined her mastery of curved piecing, machine quilting, and three-dimensional appliqué into a striking wallhanging. The interlocking Wedding Rings adorned with another symbol of love—the rose—make this a quilt that no true romantic can resist. In addition to the appliqué, machine stipple quilting provides further visual interest to the quilt.

BEFORE YOU BEGIN

This quilt is an intricate combination of pieced Wedding Rings and appliqué. We have provided yardage requirements and cutting instructions for two sizes, the wallhanging pictured and a queen-size quilt. Because the three-dimensional appliqué is added after the entire quilt top is pieced, we have not given specific numbers of flower pieces to cut for the queen size. You may prefer to add flowers and vines just around the outer rings so you won't have to maneuver your way to the center of the quilt top to appliqué. Or you may want the challenge of appliquéing across the entire surface. Therefore, we have provided guidelines for yardage and cutting, but we'll leave the specifics up to you.

Read through the entire project directions before beginning, and refer to "Wedding Ring Basics," beginning on page 104, if you need additional information on piecing your quilt top.

You will need to make both Wedding Ring templates and flower templates for this quilt. Use templates A, B, C, D, and E on page 21 to piece the quilt top. The flower templates are on pages 48–49. For more information on making and using templates, see page 116 in "Quiltmaking Basics."

Quilt Sizes		
	Wallhanging (shown)	Queen
Finished Quilt Size	39" × 48½"	96" × 105½"
Finished Ring Size	15"	15"
Number of Rings	12	90
Number of Pieced Arcs	62	398

Materials		
	Wallhanging	Queen
Beige	1½ yards	9⅞ yards
Tan	½ yard	1¼ yards
Taupe	⅓ yard	2 yards
Brown	1¼ yards	3½ yards
Pink	⅜ yard	1¼ yards
Rose	⅓ yard	2 yards
Maroon	1¾ yards	4½ yards
Mauve	½ yard	2½ yards
Dark mauve	⅓ yard	2 yards
Rose print	⅓ yard	¾ yard
Backing	2¾ yards	8¾ yards
Batting	46" × 56"	103" × 113"
Binding	½ yard	⅞ yard

NOTE: Yardages are based on 44/45-inch-wide fabrics that are at least 42 inches wide after preshrinking.

Cutting Chart

Fabric	Used For	Piece	Number of Pieces	
			Wallhanging	Queen
Beige	Background	A	12	90
	Melons	B	31	199
Tan	Connecting diamonds	C	31	199
Pink	Connecting diamonds	C	31	199
Rose	Arcs	D	62	398
Maroon	Arcs	E	62	398
Mauve	Arcs	E	62	398
Dark mauve	Arcs	E	62	398
Brown	Arcs	E	62	398
Taupe	Arcs	D reverse	62	398

Fabric	Used For	Strip Width	Number of Strips	
			Wallhanging	Queen
Maroon	Borders	6"	4	10

NOTE: You will also need to cut the flower pieces using the patterns on pages 48–49. Each pattern piece indicates the number of pieces to cut from each fabric for the wallhanging.

CHOOSING FABRICS

The quiltmaker selected solid hand-dyed fabrics for her quilt. The surface of the quilt changes from shades of rose to greenish tans, with an occasional splash of light pink to brighten the quilt. Only one print was used to add detail to the petals of the three-dimensional roses. This print was also used for the quilt binding.

You can buy commercially dyed fabrics in the same color range or in another color scheme. Look for complementary colors in muted shades if you want to achieve the soft mood of this quilt.

If you prefer to use hand-dyed fabrics but don't have access to them in your area, you'll find source information on page 106 in "Wedding Ring Basics."

CUTTING

All measurements include ¼-inch seam allowances. Referring to the Cutting Chart, cut the required number of pieces for your quilt size. For the floral appliqué for the wallhanging, you will find the number of pieces to cut from each fabric listed on the individual pattern pieces.

You will also need to cut 1⅛-inch-wide bias strips from the brown fabric to make the vines. The bias strips should be about 20 inches long. For the wallhanging, you will need about 15 bias strips. The number needed for the queen-size quilt will depend on whether you appliqué just around the edges or across the entire quilt top. If you appliqué the entire top, you will need about sixty 20-inch bias strips. If you appliqué only the outer edges, you will need about 25 bias strips.

Note: Cut and piece one sample block before cutting all of the fabric for the quilt.

PIECING THE ARCS

Step 1. Stack the D, D reverse, and E pieces in separate piles, according to color. Begin each pieced arc with a rose D. To the right of it, sew a maroon E, then a mauve E, a dark mauve E, and a brown E; end with a taupe D reverse piece. As you sew, be sure pieces are oriented so that curves arch in the same direction, so your finished arc looks like the one in **Diagram 1**. Gently press seams to one side, taking care not to stretch the unit. Repeat, assembling all the arcs required for your quilt.

Diagram 1

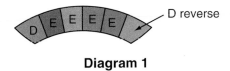

Sew Quick

You can speed up the process of making pieced arcs by chain piecing the segments. For example, sew all rose D pieces to maroon E pieces. Then sew the mauve and dark mauve E pieces together. Then join the pairs together. See page 117 in "Quiltmaking Basics" for more information about chain piecing.

Step 2. Center and sew one pieced arc to one side of each B melon, as shown in **Diagram 2**. For more detailed information on assembling the curved pieces common to most Double Wedding Ring quilts, refer to page 107 in "Wedding Ring Basics." Press the seams toward the melon. You will use half of the pieced arcs for this step.

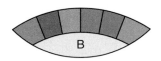

Diagram 2

Step 3. Sew a tan C piece to the light rose D end of the remaining arcs. Sew a pink C piece to

the taupe D reverse piece at the opposite end of each arc, as shown in **Diagram 3**. Gently press the seams in the same direction as the other seams in the arc.

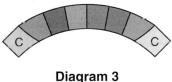

Diagram 3

Step 4. Center and sew these longer pieced arcs to the arc/melon units, as shown in **Diagram 4**. Press all seams toward the melons.

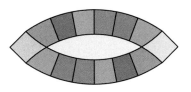

Diagram 4

ASSEMBLING THE QUILT TOP

Step 1. Use a design wall or other flat surface to lay out the completed arc/melon units and the A background pieces in rows, as shown in the **Partial Assembly Diagram**. Note that the orientation of arc/melon units changes from row to row, so refer to the diagram or the photograph on page 40 for directional placement of the pink and tan tips of the arc/melon units.

Partial Assembly Diagram

For the wallhanging, you will have four horizontal rows of three rings each. For the queen-size quilt, you will have ten horizontal rows each of nine rings each.

Step 2. Sew the units into horizontal rows. You will need to start and stop stitching ¼ inch from each end of the arcs as you attach them to the beige background pieces. Refer to page 107 in "Wedding Ring Basics" for more details on piecing curves.

Step 3. The assembled rings are appliquéd to a preassembled border unit. For the wallhanging, trim two of the 6-inch wide maroon strips to 37½ inches for the side borders and trim the others to 39 inches for the top and bottom borders. For the queen-size quilt, you will first need to piece the strips together. Then cut two 94½-inch borders for the sides and two 105½-inch borders for the top and bottom.

Step 4. Beginning at any corner, sew a side border to a top or bottom border, placing the right sides together and aligning the outer edges. Repeat to assemble the border unit shown in **Diagram 5.** Press the seams open.

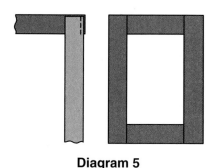

Diagram 5

Step 5. Center the completed quilt top on the border unit. Pin or baste the rings in place, then hand or machine appliqué the outer ring edges to the border, turning under the edges of rings as you work. See the **Wallhanging Diagram.** Refer to page 109 for details on the freezer paper method that can be used for this step. When the appliqué is complete, trim the excess border fabric from beneath the rings to eliminate bulk.

Appliquéing the Flowers

To plan the position of the roses, buds, and leaves, refer to the photo on page 40, or make photocopies of the **Wedding Ring Color Plan** on page 111 and sketch in flowers and vines until you are happy with your layout. Making extra bias vine will give you more flexibility to experiment with the design in progress.

Making the Bias Vines

The vine winding through the rings of this quilt appears to be continuous. However, since there are so many junctions of leaves, blossoms, and buds, you can use shorter, easier-to-handle lengths, then hide their raw edges under the appliquéd shapes. We recommend you use a ¼-inch bias bar to make these long, narrow stems.

Step 1. Cut 1⅛-inch-wide bias strips from the brown fabric. Each strip should be at least 20 inches long so you can position graceful curves between appliquéd pieces on your quilt.

Step 2. Fold the strip in half lengthwise, with *wrong* sides together. Press lightly to hold the edges of the fabric together as you stitch. To avoid stretching, do not move the iron back and forth—use an up-and-down motion. Sew the raw edges together using a ¼-inch seam allowance. Trim the seam allowance to approximately ⅛ inch.

Step 3. Insert a ¼-inch bias bar into the tube you've just created, turning the tube slightly to center the seam along the flat edge of the bar. Press the seam allowance to one side, dampening the fabric with water or a bit of spray starch to achieve crisp edges. Trim the seam allowance a bit more if it is too bulky.

Step 4. Flip the tube over, and check to be sure that the seam will be hidden when the strip is appliquéd to the quilt. When you are satisfied with the appearance, press the top side of the tube and remove the bias bar. If your vines are particularly long, you will have to slide the bias bar along the inside of the fabric tube to press the entire length before removing the bar.

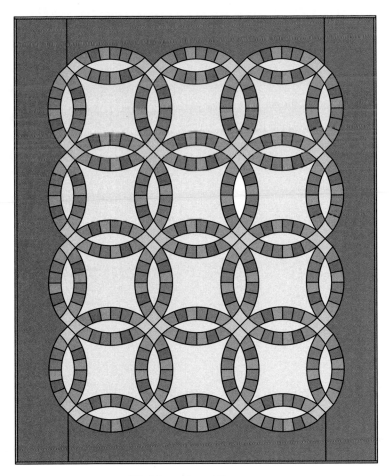

Wallhanging Diagram

Step 5. Position the stems as shown in the photograph on page 40 or as determined by your own design. Make sure junctions with raw edges will be hidden by leaves, buds, or blossoms. You can appliqué the stems to the quilt now or after all other designs have been added.

Making the Roses and Leaves

Step 1. For each rose, you will need one background F piece from the rose print fabric. Use the technique of your choice to prepare these pieces for appliqué, referring to page 118 in "Quiltmaking Basics" for more information on appliqué.

Step 2. Each rose also requires two two-sided G petals and three two-sided H petals. Place your

petal fabrics (rose print and maroon) *right* sides together, then make two tracings of template G and three tracings of template H onto the wrong side of the lightest fabric. Be sure to leave at least $1/4$ inch between tracings for seam allowances. Do not cut out the shapes yet.

Step 3. To avoid shifting, press the two petal fabrics together or use a few pins to hold them in place. Machine stitch through both fabrics, sewing directly on the marked lines and backstitching at the beginning and end of seams. Be sure to leave an opening at the bottom of each piece, as indicated on the templates. Cut out all shapes approximately $1/8$ inch from the stitching, then clip into the curves. Turn the petals right side out and smooth the seams. Gather the petals slightly with a basting stitch along the open edges. Secure the threads.

Step 4. For the center of each rose, you will need to make a rosebud using template I. The quilt shown has rosebuds cut from a variety of the quilt fabrics. Trace your required number of rosebuds onto your selected fabrics and cut them out. Fold each circle in half, with *wrong* sides together.

Make another fold across the straight folded edge, as shown in **Diagram 6**, angling the fold so that the right edge is folded under more than the left edge. With the second fold away from you, fold each side of the half circle diagonally toward the middle, overlapping the sides. Pin to keep the folds in place. Gather the bottom of the bud, using a basting stitch and pulling the threads tight. Secure the threads.

Fold circle in half.   Fold top edge.   Fold sides toward center. Gather this lower edge.

Diagram 6

Step 5. Pin or baste the flower background in place on the quilt, then appliqué it. Position two G petals, darker fabric face up, with their upper edges slightly below the top of the flower background, then tack them to the background at their bases. Center a rosebud between the two petals, tacking it to the background at its base. When tacking the bud and petals in place, do not let your needle come through the top layers of fabric. See **Diagram 7.**

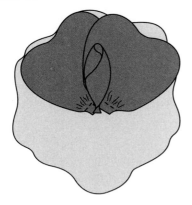

Diagram 7

Step 6. Position an H petal beneath the bud and sew it in place along its base. Position one of the remaining H petals to the lower left of the bud. Tuck under the lower unfinished petal edges and appliqué the petal in place, leaving the top edge free. Repeat with the last H petal, positioning it to the lower right of the bud. See **Diagram 8.** Fold down the top edges of petals as desired, taking more tacking stitches through the back layer of fabric to hold petals in place as necessary.

Note: Edges that will be overlapped by another piece of fabric should not be turned under, as this will just add bulk to your roses. Take as many stitches in the bottom layers of petals as necessary to secure them before adding outer layers.

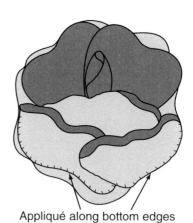

Appliqué along bottom edges

Diagram 8

Step 7. Repeat Steps 1 through 6 for the remaining roses.

Step 8. Use the technique of your choice to prepare the J and K leaves for appliqué. Arrange leaves as desired and appliqué to the quilt top.

Step 9. Make the rosebuds as described in Step 4. Position and secure the buds to the quilt top. Use template L and the method of your choice to prepare the calyxes (bases) for appliqué. Position them over the lower portions of the buds, as shown in **Diagram 9**, and appliqué them. For extra dimension, you can stuff the lower half of the calyxes with a bit of batting.

Diagram 9

QUILTING AND FINISHING

Step 1. Mark the quilt top for quilting. The quilt shown was machine stipple quilted within the melons and ring backgrounds; the rings were also quilted in the ditch. A line was quilted along the center of the leaves to give them depth and a more natural appearance. Clusters of leaves on vines were quilted in the borders. You can use appliqué templates J and K to trace the leaf

shapes, or you can make a variety of your own leaves.

Step 2. Regardless of which quilt size you've chosen to make, the backing will have to be pieced. For the wallhanging, cut the backing fabric into two equal lengths, and trim the selvages. From one length, cut two 8-inch-wide panels. Sew a narrow panel to each side of the full-width panel, as shown in **Diagram 10**. Press the seams open.

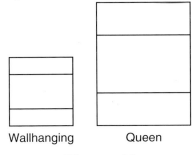

Wallhanging   Queen

Diagram 10

Step 3. For the queen-size quilt, cut the backing fabric into three equal lengths, and trim the selvages. Cut a 37-inch-wide panel from two of the lengths, and sew one to each side of the remaining full-width panel, as shown. Press the seams open.

Step 4. Layer the backing, batting, and quilt top, and baste. Quilt as desired.

Step 5. Make and attach double-fold binding, referring to page 121 in "Quiltmaking Basics" for more information. To calculate the amount of binding needed for the quilt size you are making, add the length of the four sides of the quilt plus 9 inches.

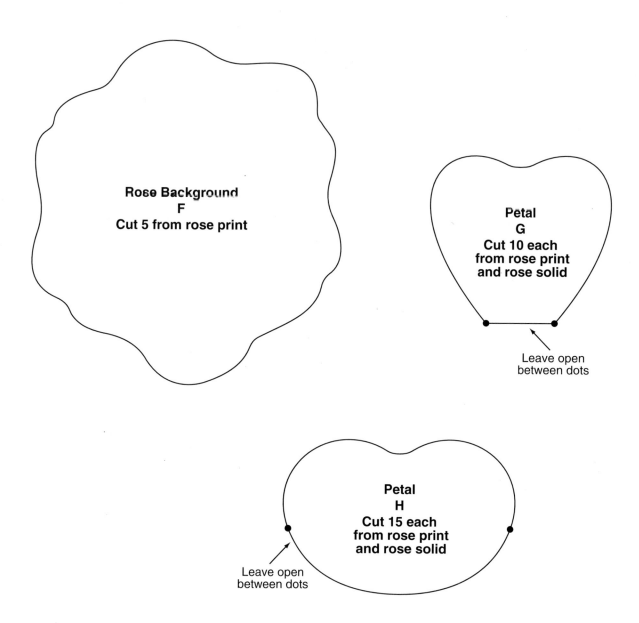

Rose Background
F
Cut 5 from rose print

Petal
G
Cut 10 each
from rose print
and rose solid

Leave open
between dots

Petal
H
Cut 15 each
from rose print
and rose solid

Leave open
between dots

Patterns are finished size.
Add seam allowances when cutting fabric.

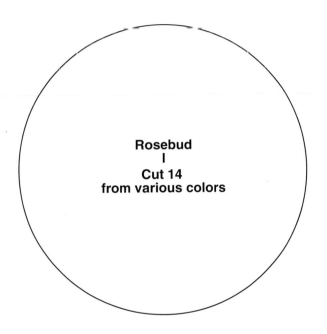

Rosebud
I
Cut 14
from various colors

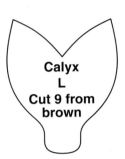

Calyx
L
Cut 9 from
brown

Leaf
K
Cut 5 from brown

Leaf
J
Cut 49 from brown
or taupe

CRAZY WEDDING RING

Skill Level: *Intermediate*

Joanne Winn's Crazy Wedding Ring wallhanging creatively combines the best of the old with the best of the new. Scraps of fabrics sewn to foundation pieces in the crazy-quilting style popular in the Victorian age are enhanced with decorative stitching. Joanne's updated technique lets you take advantage of the wonderful decorative machine stitches and threads available today to create a vintage look. The real surprise is that the curved piecing associated with a Wedding Ring quilt has been completely eliminated! The crazy-pieced melons are appliquéd by hand or machine to a continuous background.

BEFORE YOU BEGIN

Unlike traditional Wedding Ring quilts, the Crazy Wedding Ring requires only one template, the melon. However, we recommend that you make two plastic templates, one that includes the seam allowance and one that doesn't. The melon pattern is on page 57. The template with the ¼-inch seam allowance will be used for tracing paper foundation pieces. The finished-size template will be used to mark the turn-under line for appliqué. Refer to page 116 in "Quiltmaking Basics" for more information on making and using templates.

Freezer paper, blank newsprint, onionskin, and heavy tracing paper all work well for foundation piecing, and they can be torn away easily after your pieces are sewn. Trace and cut out 49 melons for the wallhanging or 220 melons for the queen-size quilt.

CHOOSING FABRICS

Both the borders and melons in this quilt are crazy pieced. For this technique, an assortment of many fabrics will give you the best results. Fat eighths, fat quarters, scraps, and precut squares will all work well. Choose solids, small-scale prints, prints with contrast, and large, splashy prints that resemble tapestry. Don't worry as much about color as about the variety of fabrics. This

Quilt Sizes

	Wallhanging (shown)	Queen
Finished Quilt Size	47½" × 55½"	99½" × 99½"
Finished Ring Size	11"	11"
Number of Melons	49	220

Materials

	Wallhanging	Queen
Ivory for background	1⅜ yards	7½ yards
Assorted fabric scraps for patchwork and binding	2¾ yards	6½ yards
Muslin foundation for borders	⅔ yard	1⅝ yards
Backing	3⅛ yards	9⅓ yards
Batting	55" × 63"	108" × 108"
Machine embroidery thread		
Freezer paper or tracing paper for foundations		

NOTE: Yardages are based on 44/45-inch-wide fabrics that are at least 42 inches wide after preshrinking.

51

quilt was made with many dark, muted fabrics of similiar color value, but the random addition of both light and vibrant pieces will give the quilt pizzazz.

You will also need to choose several threads for machine embroidery. You may use traditional cotton or cotton-covered polyester threads, or try rayon threads that highlight the colors in your fabrics to make a more dramatic statement.

If you would like to experiment with different colors for your Crazy Wedding Ring quilt, photocopy the **Wedding Ring Color Plan** on page 111 and use crayons or colored pencils to plan your own color scheme.

CUTTING

The yardage requirements given are estimates and will likely vary depending on the size of your crazy pieces and waste from trimming excess seam allowances when piecing. The method of crazy piecing requires cutting as you go rather than pre-cutting pieces. Only the background fabric and border foundation pieces will need to be cut to a predetermined size. These pieces will be cut later, when you are ready to assemble the quilt top.

PIECING THE MELONS

Step 1. Choose a fabric to begin your first melon, and cut an approximately 3 × 3½-inch rectangle from it. Position the piece right side up on your paper foundation, as shown in **Diagram 1**. A portion of the fabric may extend beyond the edge of your foundation. This excess fabric will be trimmed away later.

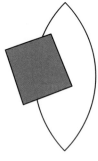

Diagram 1

Sew Easy

If you are using freezer paper as your foundation, be sure to sew the fabric to the matte (nonshiny) side of the paper. Otherwise, when you flip and press your pieces, your iron will stick to the plastic coating on the paper. To keep the coated side from sticking to your ironing board when you press, simply lay a scrap of muslin on your ironing board.

Step 2. Choose another fabric and cut a rectangle from it, making sure that one side is about as long as the right edge of your first rectangle. Position the rectangle right side down along the right edge of the first piece, matching the raw edges, as shown in **Diagram 2A**. Using a ¼-inch seam allowance, sew the two pieces to the foundation paper. Flip the second fabric over so both pieces are right side up, as shown in **2B**. Press the seam lightly after the addition of this and each new piece.

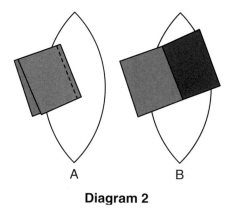

Diagram 2

Step 3. Choose a third fabric and cut a piece from it that is large enough to cover the top portion of the melon. Position it right side down, aligned flush with the top raw edge of the first two pieces, as shown in **Diagram 3A**. Stitch the layers together with a ¼-inch seam allowance, then flip the new piece so it is right side up. See **3B**.

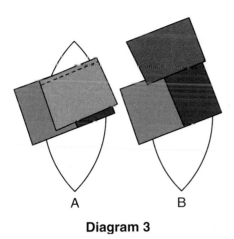

A   B

Diagram 3

Sew Easy

To add decorative machine stitching between pieces, it is best to do it after each seam. Otherwise, the edges of the seam will be covered by more pieces, making it harder to stitch a neat, stable line. By stitching before your next piece is added, the starting and stopping points of the stitching will be covered by consecutive pieces.

Step 4. The fourth fabric will cover the remaining section of the melon, so cut a piece that will cover the foundation after the piece is flipped into place. Position the piece right side down, with the bottom edge flush with the edge of pieces 1 and 2. Stitch, then flip the piece right side up. Your melon should now resemble **Diagram 4.**

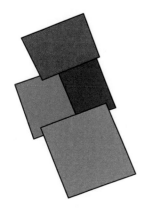

Diagram 4

Step 5. For appliquéing, you will need to mark the finished-size melon shape on your crazy-pieced melon. If you plan to use the freezer paper method described on page 109 in "Wedding Ring Basics," turn the melon over and trace the finished-size template onto the freezer paper foundation. Trim away the excess fabric to the outside line, then trim the freezer paper to the inside line, as shown in **Diagram 5.** Press the fabric seam allowance toward the freezer paper.

If you plan to do needle-turn appliqué, first trim away the excess fabric from your foundation piece. Then trace the finished-size melon onto the right side of the fabric. You may trim the seam allowance to a scant ¼ inch from the drawn line if you prefer.

If you are using decorative stitching, don't forget to add this along the seams of the last pieces you added. When all stitching is complete, remove the foundation paper.

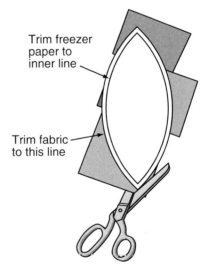

Trim freezer paper to inner line

Trim fabric to this line

Diagram 5

Step 6. Repeat Steps 1 through 5 to assemble 49 melons for the wallhanging or 220 melons for the queen-size quilt.

Remember that no two melons are exactly alike, as shown in the photograph on page 50. The instructions give an example of one way to position your fabrics for sewing. You may choose to use triangles or other shapes for some of your pieces.

Some of your melons may have more pieces than the one illustrated here. Just remember that each new piece should overlap all outside edges of the fabrics it is being sewn to.

PREPARING THE MELONS FOR APPLIQUÉ

The melons will all be appliquéd to a solid background, so the outer seam allowance of each must be turned under. See page 109 in "Wedding Ring Basics" for a suggested technique to help you prepare accurately shaped melons.

ASSEMBLING THE QUILT TOP

Step 1. For the wallhanging, trim the $1\frac{3}{8}$-yard piece of solid ivory background fabric to $40\frac{1}{2} \times 48\frac{1}{2}$ inches. The background for the queen-size quilt must be $88\frac{1}{2}$ inches square, so it will have to be pieced. Cut the $7\frac{1}{2}$-yard piece of solid ivory fabric crosswise into three equal panels, and trim all of the selvages. Choose one panel for the center section of the background and measure its width. Subtract that width from $88\frac{1}{2}$ to determine the remaining width necessary. Divide the result by two and add $\frac{1}{2}$ inch for seam allowances.

Using a 42-inch center panel as an example: $88\frac{1}{2} - 42 = 46\frac{1}{2} \div 2 = 23\frac{1}{4} + \frac{1}{2} = 23\frac{3}{4}$ inches.

Trim the remaining two panels to the width you just calculated. Sew a narrow panel to each lengthwise side of the full-width panel and press the seams open. Trim the full-size background piece to $88\frac{1}{2}$ inches long.

Step 2. In order to position the melons correctly, you must accurately mark the background. Draw a grid with a pencil or other removable marker that reflects the distance between melon centers. To do so, draw a horizontal and vertical line beginning at the upper left corner of your background, each beginning 4 inches from the outer edge of the fabric. Continue drawing horizontal and vertical lines, parallel to and 8 inches away from the first lines, as shown in **Diagram 6**.

For the wallhanging, draw five vertical lines and six horizontal lines. For the queen-size quilt, your grid should have 11 vertical and 11 horizontal lines. By starting your grid 4 inches from the edge, you will end up with a $2\frac{1}{2}$-inch border of background fabric remaining around the outside edge of the quilt top once the melons are centered over the grid lines.

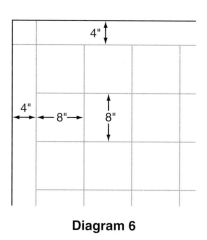

Diagram 6

Sew Easy

Instead of marking a grid on the background fabric, you may want to press your fabric into rows the width of the grid. Measure and mark the folds, then press the fabric accordion style to define the grid.

Step 3. Use a design wall or other flat surface to position the melons on the grid, referring to the **Wallhanging Diagram** on page 56. Hold the melons in place temporarily with a pin in case you want to move them around. The points of each melon should align with your drawn lines, as shown in **Diagram 7**. Continue adding melons until you are pleased with the layout, then appliqué them to the background.

For the queen-size quilt, it might be more manageable to appliqué a few rows at a time. If you

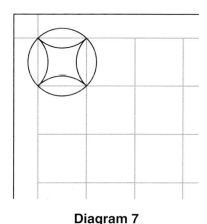

Diagram 7

decided to use the freezer paper appliqué method, remember to remove the paper after appliquéing each melon.

········Sew Quick········

You may find it easier to fuse the melons to your background using lightweight fusible web as an alternative to the appliqué method described on page 109 in "Wedding Ring Basics." This method is quick and easy, and it is particularly suitable for a wallhanging that won't be handled as much as a bed quilt. Use the finished-size template to trace melons onto the fusible web. Cut them out and follow the manufacturer's directions for fusing. After fusing the melons to the background, you can use decorative stitches along the edges to secure them.

MAKING AND ATTACHING THE BORDERS

The quilt borders are also pieced on a foundation in the same random-piecing manner as the melons. We recommend that you use a fabric foundation instead of paper for the borders. The fabric foundation will remain permanently in the quilt, giving it extra stability.

Step 1. For the wallhanging, cut muslin border strips 4 inches wide. For the queen-size quilt, cut border strips 6 inches wide. To determine the length of the side borders, measure the length of your quilt top, taking the measurement through the vertical center of the quilt rather than along the sides. Add approximately 1½ inches to that measurement, and cut (or piece together) two long muslin strips to this length. Measure the width of the quilt in a similar manner, adding two times the width of the side borders plus 1½ inches. Cut or piece together two muslin foundation strips to this length.

Use the crazy-piecing technique to cover the muslin foundations, adding decorative stitching as you go, if desired. Trim the completed side borders to the exact length of your quilt measurement.

Step 2. Fold one side border in half crosswise and crease. Unfold it and position it right side down along one side of your quilt top, with the crease at the horizontal midpoint. Pin at the midpoint and ends first, then along the length of the entire side, easing in fullness if necessary. Sew the border to the quilt top using a ¼-inch seam allowance. Repeat on the opposite side of the quilt.

Step 3. Trim the top and bottom borders to the width of your quilt. Fold the top border in half crosswise and crease. Unfold it and position it right side down along one end of your quilt top, with the crease at the vertical midpoint. Pin at the midpoint and ends first, then along the length of the entire side, easing in fullness if necessary. Sew the border to the quilt top using a ¼-inch seam allowance. Repeat on the bottom of the quilt.

QUILTING AND FINISHING

Step 1. Mark the quilt top for quilting. The quilt shown was machine quilted with clear nylon thread in the ditch of each crazy piece. In addition, an undulating feather border was quilted in the background fabric between the outer rows of

Wallhanging Diagram

rings and the crazy quilt border. The center of each ring was quilted with a flower surrounded by four leaves.

Step 2. To piece the backing for the wall-hanging, cut the backing fabric in half, and trim the selvages. Cut two 12-inch-wide panels from one segment, and sew a narrow panel to each side of the full-width panel, as shown in **Diagram 8.** Press the seams open.

Step 3. To piece the backing for the queen-size quilt, cut the backing fabric into three equal lengths, and trim the selvages. Cut a 32-inch-wide

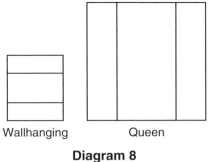

Wallhanging   Queen

Diagram 8

panel from two of the pieces, and sew one of these to each side of the remaining full-width piece, as shown. Press the seams open.

Step 4. Layer the quilt top, batting, and backing, and baste the layers together. Quilt as desired.

Step 5. The quilt shown has a pieced binding, made from scraps of the fabrics used in the quilt. Referring to the directions on page 121 in "Quiltmaking Basics," make straight-grain double-fold binding, piecing together short strips of a variety of fabrics. The length of your strips can vary, but they should all be the same width (about 2½ inches). Keep adding strips until you have the length needed to bind your entire quilt.

To calculate the approximate number of inches of binding needed for the quilt size you are making, add the length of the four sides of the quilt plus 9 inches.

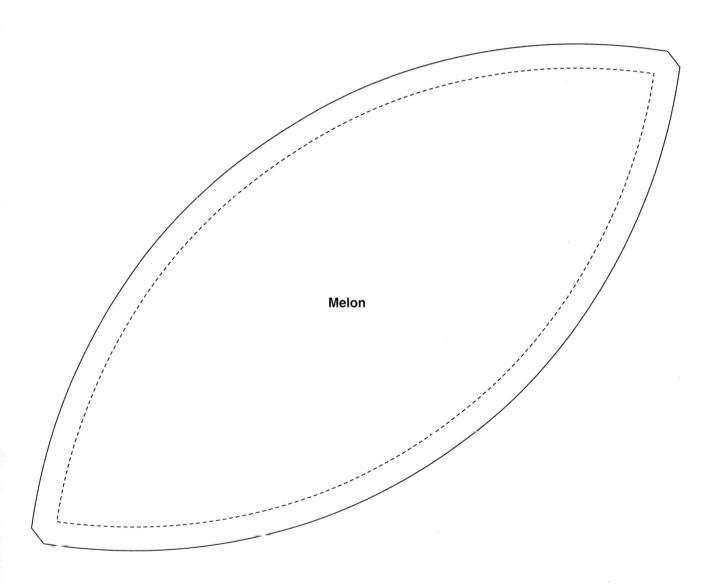

Melon

RED-AND-WHITE
WEDDING RING

Skill Level: *Intermediate*

*P*ieced in the late 1920s or early 1930s, this striking double-size quilt is quite unusual because of its two-color scheme. Most Wedding Ring quilts from that era were made from scraps of many colors. Another striking feature is the narrow pieces used in each arc, which add up to twice as many pieces per arc as there are in many of today's Wedding Ring quilts. You may also notice that the red and white borders are a slightly different color than the rest of the quilt, suggesting, perhaps, that the quilt wasn't finished by the original maker but by someone who inherited it and wanted it to have straight sides!

BEFORE YOU BEGIN

In addition to piecing curves, this quilt involves appliquéing the quilt top to a background so that straight borders can be added. One benefit of adding the borders is that you will not have to attach binding around the rings.

If this is your first Wedding Ring quilt, be sure to read through the project directions, as well as "Wedding Ring Basics," beginning on page 104, before starting. Although each project in this book contains specific information unique to its assembly, many aspects of construction are similar from quilt to quilt.

You will need to make templates for pattern pieces A, B, C, and D on pages 64–65. For information on making and using templates, see page 116 in "Quiltmaking Basics."

CHOOSING FABRICS

The quiltmaker chose to use two starkly contrasting solids for her quilt—bright red and crisp white. Whether you choose this same vibrant combination, a more subdued blue-and-white plan, or a multicolor design, be sure to purchase enough yardage at the start. It is difficult to match solid cottons from different dye lots.

This quilt could also be made with prints. Just keep in mind that the pieces in the arcs are narrower than in most Wedding Ring quilts, so small-scale prints would work better than large ones.

To plan your own color scheme for the quilt, photocopy the **Wedding Ring Color Plan** on page 111, and use crayons or colored pencils to experiment with different color options.

Quilt Sizes		
	Double (shown)	King
Finished Quilt Size	72½" × 84½"	96½" × 108½"
Finished Ring Size	18"	18"
Number of Rings	20	42
Number of Pieced Arcs	98	194

Materials		
	Double	King
White solid	6½ yards	12¼ yards
Red solid	3¾ yards	6⅝ yards
Backing	5¼ yards	9 yards
Batting	81" × 93"	105" × 117"
Binding	⅝ yard	⅞ yard

NOTE: Yardages are based on 44/45-inch-wide fabrics that are at least 42 inches wide after preshrinking.

Cutting Chart

Fabric	Used For	Piece	Number of Pieces	
			Double	King
White	Background	A	20	42
	Melons	B	49	97
	Arcs	C	588	1,164
	Connecting diamonds	D	49	97
Red	Arcs	C	588	1,164
	Connecting diamonds	D	49	97

Fabric	Used For	Strip Width	Number of Strips	
			Double	King
White	Second border	1½"	8	11
	Fourth border	1¾"	8	11
	Appliqué background	6"	6	9
Red	First border	1½"	8	11
	Third border	1½"	8	11
	Outer border	2¼"	8	11

CUTTING

All measurements include ¼-inch seam allowances. Referring to the Cutting Chart, cut the required number of pieces for your quilt size.

Note: Cut and piece one sample ring before cutting all of the fabric for the quilt.

PIECING THE ARCS

Step 1. Sew six red and six white C pieces together to form an arc, beginning with a red piece and alternating colors, as shown in **Diagram 1**. Press the seams toward the red pieces, being careful not to stretch the unit. Repeat, constructing half of the pieced arcs required for your quilt size— 49 for the double size or 97 for the king size.

Diagram 1

Step 2. Pin a pieced arc to one side of each B melon, matching centers, then stitch them together, as shown in **Diagram 2**. For more information about piecing the curved seams found in traditional Double Wedding Ring quilts, see page 107 in "Wedding Ring Basics." Press the seams toward the melons.

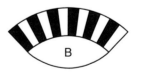

Diagram 2

Step 3. To make the rest of the arcs, sew six white and six red C pieces together to form each arc. Begin with a white piece and alternate colors. Then sew a red D piece to the left of the arc and a white D piece to the right of the arc, as shown in **Diagram 3**. Carefully press the seams toward the red pieces. Repeat this step until you've assembled the remaining pieced arcs required for the size quilt you are making.

Diagram 3

Step 4. Sew each arc to the unsewn side of the arc/melon units, as shown in **Diagram 4**. Press the seams toward the melons.

Diagram 4

ASSEMBLING THE QUILT TOP

Step 1. Use a design wall or other flat surface to lay out the completed arc/melon units and the background A pieces in rows, as shown in the **Partial Assembly Diagram**. Note that the orientation of the arcs changes from row to row, so refer to the diagram or the photograph on page 58 for directional placement of the red and white D pieces at the tips of the arc/melon units.

Partial Assembly Diagram

Step 2. Sew the units together into horizontal rows. You will need to start and stop stitching 1/4 inch from each end of the arcs as you attach them to the white background pieces. Refer to page 109 in "Wedding Ring Basics" for more details on sewing rings into rows.

Step 3. To complete the quilt top, sew the rows together, starting and stopping your seams 1/4 inch from the end of each arc.

Step 4. Before the borders can be added, the outer edges of the quilt are first appliquéd to a preassembled background unit. To make the background unit, piece together the 6-inch white strips for the quilt top background to obtain the lengths needed for your size quilt. Measure the width of your quilt top through the center. Cut two white background strips to this measurement minus 10 inches. Then measure the length of the quilt top through the vertical center. Cut two white background strips to this measurement plus 2 inches.

Step 5. Beginning at any corner, sew a side background strip to a top or bottom background strip, placing right sides together and aligning outer edges. Repeat to assemble the background unit shown in **Diagram 5**. Press the seams open.

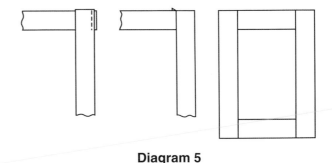

Diagram 5

Step 6. Center the completed quilt top on the background. Pin or baste it in place, then appliqué the top to the background around the outer edges, turning under the edges of the rings as you work. Refer to page 109 in "Wedding Ring Basics" for information about the freezer paper appliqué method you can use for this step. When the appliquéing is complete, trim away excess fabric from the inner

Sew Easy

Since the outer curved edges of the rings are slightly bias, there's always a chance of stretching the rings out of shape as you baste them to the background. To prevent this, run a row of hand basting stitches around the perimeter of the quilt *before* basting it to the background. This stitching, which should be about ¹⁄₂ to ⁵⁄₈ inch from the edge, will help to stabilize the quilt edges without getting in the way of the seam allowance you will be turning under.

portion of the background as necessary to eliminate bulk.

ADDING THE BORDERS

Step 1. To determine the length needed for the side borders, measure the quilt top vertically through the center. To this measurement, add two times the finished width of the borders (6 inches × 2) plus approximately 5 inches. This is the length you need to make the side borders. In the same manner, measure the quilt top horizontally through the center, and calculate the length of the top and bottom borders.

Step 2. Sew the first (inner) red border strips together end to end to make the top, bottom, and two side borders in the lengths you calculated. Do the same with the strips for the remaining four borders. Be sure to keep all of the side border strips separate from the top and bottom border strips.

Step 3. Pin and sew the individual red and white border strips together to make the top, bottom, and side border units, as shown in **Diagram 6**. The innermost border is a 1¹⁄₂-inch red strip. Working outward, a 1¹⁄₂-inch white strip is next, followed by another 1¹⁄₂-inch red

strip and a 1³⁄₄-inch white strip. This unit ends with a 2¹⁄₄-inch red strip. Press all seams toward the red borders.

Diagram 6

Step 4. Pin and sew the four borders to the quilt top, with the narrow red borders on the inside, as shown in the **Double-Size Quilt Diagram.** Be sure each border is centered along the edge of the quilt it is sewn to. Refer to page 119 in "Quiltmaking Basics" for instructions on finishing the mitered corners. When preparing the miters, be sure to carefully match up the seams in adjacent borders.

QUILTING AND FINISHING

Step 1. Mark the quilt top for quilting. The quilt shown has echo quilting in the center of each ring, spaced about ³⁄₄ inch apart. The rings are also outline quilted, as are the borders.

Step 2. Regardless of which quilt size you've chosen to make, the backing will have to be pieced. To make the backing for the double-size quilt, cut the backing fabric crosswise into two equal lengths, and trim the selvages. Cut one piece in half lengthwise. Sew a narrow panel to each side of the full-width panel, as shown in **Diagram 7.** Press the seams open.

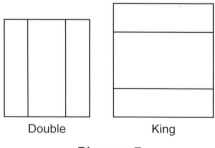

Double   King

Diagram 7

Double-Size Quilt Diagram

Step 3. For the king-size quilt, cut the backing fabric crosswise into three equal lengths, and trim the selvages. Cut a 38-inch-wide panel from two of the pieces. Sew a 38-inch panel to each side of the full-width panel, as shown. Press the seams open.

Step 4. Layer the backing, batting, and quilt top, and baste. Quilt as desired.

Step 5. Make and attach double-fold binding, referring to page 121 in "Quiltmaking Basics" for more information. To calculate the amount of binding needed for your quilt size, add the length of the four sides of the quilt plus 9 inches. The total is the approximate number of inches of binding you will need.

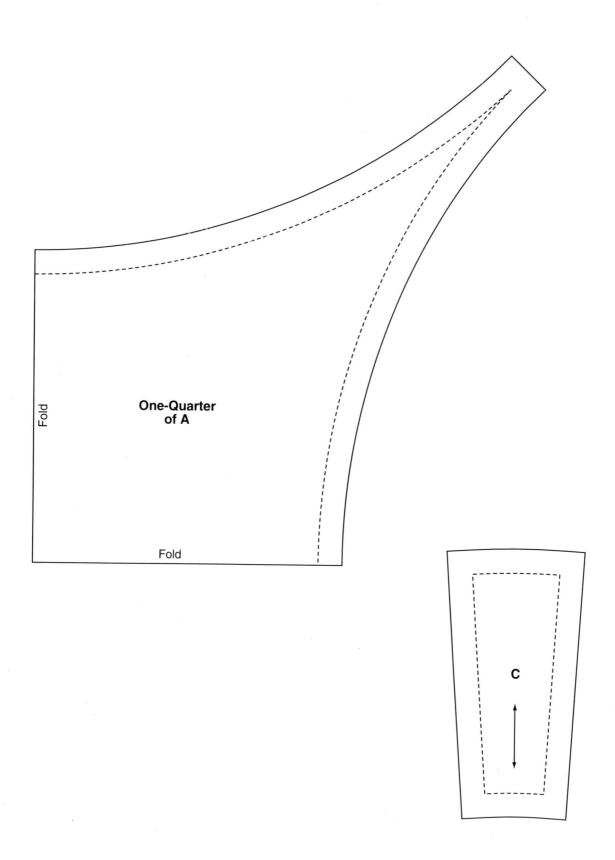

**One-Quarter
of A**

Fold

Fold

C

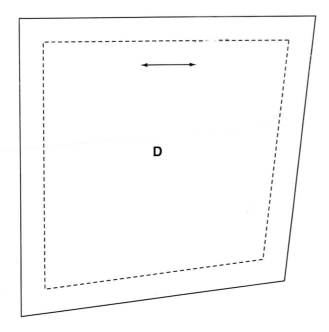

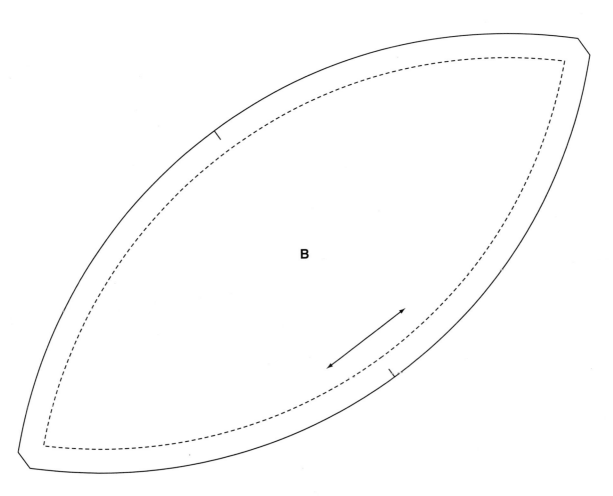

SPIDERWEBS AND DEWDROPS

Skill Level: *Intermediate*

T his spectacular wallhanging sparkles in the light, thanks to metallic spiderweb quilting and iridescent beading. Quiltmaker Susan Stein confesses to having made this quilt, which is quite lovely in its own right, several years prior to deciding to add the embellishments, which truly make the quilt a knockout.

BEFORE YOU BEGIN

We recommend that you read through all of these directions, as well as "Wedding Ring Basics," beginning on page 104, before starting this project, especially if this is your first time making a Double Wedding Ring quilt. Even if you've made Wedding Ring quilts, you'll find tips and pointers throughout the book to make the process fun and rewarding.

CHOOSING FABRICS

The rings in this quilt are pieced from a gradation of solid hand-dyed fabrics, which move from warm to cool along the length of each arc. A midnight blue solid fabric is used for all other parts of the quilt. While hand-dyed fabrics add a richness to the quilt, you can achieve a similar effect with commercially dyed fabrics if hand-dyed fabrics are not available in your area. Or see page 106 for ordering information.

The vibrant pinks and teals contrast with the midnight blue to give this quilt a feel similar to that of an Amish color palette. Yet the iridescent black beads and a rainbow metallic quilting thread that highlights the colors in the rings make this quilt distinctively contemporary.

If you would like to experiment with blending shades of other colors for the arcs, such as blues into greens or pinks into purples, photocopy the **Wedding Ring Color Plan** on page 111, and use crayons or colored pencils to try different color arrangements.

Quilt Sizes

	Wallhanging (shown)	Twin
Finished Quilt Size	40½" × 40½"	72" × 93"
Finished Ring Size	15"	15"
Number of Rings	9	48
Number of Pieced Arcs	48	220

Materials

	Wallhanging	Twin
Midnight blue	2 yards	7⅝ yards
Magenta	¼ yard	⅞ yard
Rose	⅓ yard	1 yard
Lavender	⅓ yard	⅞ yard
Orchid	⅓ yard	⅞ yard
Blue	⅓ yard	⅞ yard
Teal	⅓ yard	⅞ yard
Aqua	⅓ yard	1 yard
Green	¼ yard	⅞ yard
Backing	2¾ yards	5¾ yards
Batting	48" × 48"	79" × 100"

NOTE: Yardages are based on 44/45-inch-wide fabrics that are at least 42 inches wide after preshrinking.

Cutting Chart

Fabric	Used For	Piece	Number of Pieces	
			Wallhanging	Twin
Midnight blue	Background	A	9	48
	Melons	B	24	110
Magenta	Connecting diamonds	C	24	110
Green	Connecting diamonds	C	24	110
Rose	Outer wedges of arcs	D	48	220
Lavender	Inner wedges of arcs	E	48	220
Orchid	Inner wedges of arcs	E	48	220
Blue	Inner wedges of arcs	E	48	220
Teal	Inner wedges of arcs	E	48	220
Aqua	Outer wedges of arcs	D reverse	48	220

Fabric	Used For	Strip Width	Number of Strips	
			Wallhanging	Twin
Midnight blue	Border	6"	4	8
All eight other fabrics	Binding	2½"	1 of each	1 of each

CUTTING

All measurements for cutting strips include ¼-inch seam allowances. Make templates for pieces A, B, C, D, and E from the patterns on page 21, referring to page 116 in "Quiltmaking Basics" for information about making and using templates. Then, referring to the Cutting Chart, cut the required number of pieces for your quilt size. For the border and binding, cut strips in the stated width across the full width of the fabric.

Note: Cut and piece one sample ring before cutting all of the fabric for the quilt.

PIECING THE ARCS

Step 1. Each arc is constructed from the D, D reverse, and E pieces, beginning with a rose D piece and continuing to the right along the arc in the following order: lavender E, orchid E, blue E, teal E, and aqua D reverse. As you sew, be sure pieces are oriented so that curves arch in the same direction. Gently press seams to one side, taking care not to stretch the unit. Repeat until you've assembled all of the arcs required for your quilt. Each pieced arc should look like the example shown in **Diagram 1**.

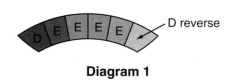

Diagram 1

Step 2. Center and sew one pieced arc to one side of each midnight blue melon, as shown in **Diagram 2**. To determine the center of the melon, fold it in half and lightly crease it. The seam between the two center E pieces marks the center of the arcs. For more specific information and tips on assembling curved pieces, refer to page 107 in "Wedding Ring Basics." Press each seam toward the melon. You will use half of the pieced arcs for this step.

Diagram 2

Step 3. Sew a magenta C piece to each end of *half* of the remaining pieced arcs. Gently press all seams in the same direction. Sew a green C piece to each end of the remaining arcs and press. You now have two types of arcs, as shown in **Diagram 3**.

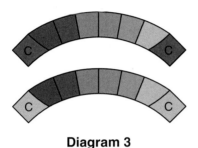

Diagram 3

····· Sew Quick ·······

Since all of the arcs are identical, assembly line piecing can make arc construction quick and easy. For example, stack all rose D pieces alongside the lavender E pieces. Pair these pieces, with right sides together, then sew them together. Then go on to the next pair, the orchid E and blue E pieces. After assembling the pairs, sew them together to form the arcs, and you'll be sure to have your colors in the right sequence.

Step 4. Center and sew the arcs to the melon units, matching the seam of the C pieces with the seam on the tip of the partially completed melons. Press all seams toward the melons. Make two stacks for the new units, one with magenta ends and one with green ends, as shown in **Diagram 4**. Again, refer to page 107 in "Wedding Ring Basics" for further explanation of sewing curved seams.

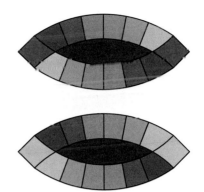

Diagram 4

ASSEMBLING THE QUILT TOP

Step 1. Sew the completed arc/melon units to the background A pieces, as shown in **Diagram 5**, leaving ¼ inch open at the beginning and end of each seam. For the wallhanging, you will have one A piece with an arc/melon unit sewn to all four sides, four A pieces with three units attached, and four A pieces with two units attached. For the twin-size quilt, you will have one A piece with arc/melon units attached to all four sides. Twelve A pieces will have units on three sides, and 35 A pieces will have two units attached. Be sure to alternate the colors of the tips from magenta to green, as shown.

Make 1 for either size.

Make 4 for wallhanging.
Make 12 for twin.

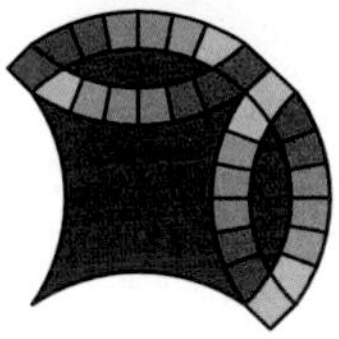

Make 4 for wallhanging.
Make 35 for twin.

Diagram 5

Step 2. Use a design wall or other flat surface to lay out the units for the wallhanging, as shown in the **Wallhanging Assembly Diagram.** For the twin-size quilt, lay out eight horizontal rows of rings, with six rings in each row. Notice that arc units with the magenta tips are all placed horizontally in the rings, while those with green tips are positioned vertically.

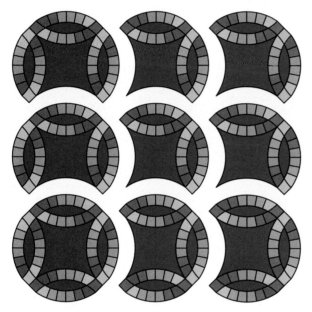

Wallhanging Assembly Diagram

Step 3. Sew units together in rows, starting and stopping seams ¼ inch from each end and backstitching. Then sew the rows together to complete the quilt top. For more assembly details, see page 109 in "Wedding Ring Basics."

MAKING AND ATTACHING THE BORDER

For either size quilt, the outside edge of the quilt center is appliquéd onto a preassembled border unit.

Step 1. For the wallhanging, trim two of the 6-inch-wide midnight border strips to 29½ inches long for the quilt sides, and trim two strips to 40½ inches long for the top and bottom borders. For the twin-size quilt, join four sets of two 6-inch-

wide border strips. Cut two of the long strips to 81½ inches for the quilt sides, and trim the other two long strips to 72 inches for the top and bottom borders.

Step 2. For either size quilt, sew a side border to a top or bottom border, placing right sides together and aligning outer edges, as shown in **Diagram 6A.** Press the seams toward the side borders. See **6B.** Repeat for all corners to assemble the entire border unit, as shown in **6C.**

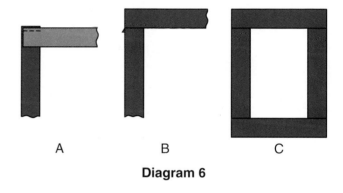

Diagram 6

Step 3. Prepare the outer rings for appliqué. Refer to page 109 in "Wedding Ring Basics" for details about the freezer paper method of preparing the ring edges. Center the completed quilt top on the border unit. Pin or baste in place, then hand or machine appliqué the top to the border around the outer rings. The **Wallhanging Diagram** shows how the completed wallhanging will look. The twin-size quilt is finished the same way but has more rings to be appliquéd. Trim away excess fabric from the inner portion of the border as necessary to eliminate excess fabric. If you use the freezer paper method, remove the paper when the appliqué is complete.

QUILTING AND FINISHING

Step 1. Mark the quilt top for quilting. The quilt shown has a glittery spiderweb, stitched with metallic thread, stretching across the midnight blue center of each ring. Midnight blue thread was used to machine quilt in the ditch around the rings and melons. The quiltmaker also used shim-

Wallhanging Diagram

mering black seed beads, staggered at ½-inch intervals, in the borders and melon of her quilt. Each bead is stitched by hand, embellishing the surface of the quilt. The beading also acts as quilting since the beads are stitched through all layers of the quilt.

Sew Easy

Metallic threads are much more brittle than cotton, polyester, or rayon threads. To avoid breaking your top thread when machine quilting, stitch a little more slowly, especially when starting out. It also helps if your thread is not taut, so turn your spool a half turn to loosen the tension before you begin to stitch.

If you wish to add beads to your quilt, construct a prepunched see-through grid to simplify the task of marking bead positions.

Step 2. To make a see-through grid, first determine the spacing you will use for bead placement and whether the beads will be positioned in matching or staggered rows. Use a ruler to determine placement points, then mark the points on a sheet of template plastic. Final template size is up to you, but a large sheet of plastic will allow you to mark more bead positions before having to reposition it. Use an ice pick, awl, or similar tool to punch through each marked hole. One-eighth-inch paper punches work well for narrow templates.

Position the template over an area that will be beaded. Use a light-color pencil to mark the fabric at each hole. Move the sheet around if necessary to mark positions, avoiding seam allowance areas in the borders. After the quilt has been quilted, sew a bead at each mark, then tie it off on the back and bury the thread ends in the batting layer.

— Sew Easy —

Instead of using an ice pick or awl to punch holes in template plastic to make a grid, try using a heated darning needle. Hold the needle with a pair of pliers so you don't burn your fingers. You'll find that the hot tip of the needle will poke through the template plastic easily.

Step 3. Regardless of which quilt size you've chosen to make, the backing will have to be pieced.

For the wallhanging, cut the backing fabric into two equal lengths, and trim the selvages. Cut a 32-inch-wide panel from one length and a 16-inch-wide panel from the other length. Sew the two panels together, as shown in **Diagram 7**. Press the seam open.

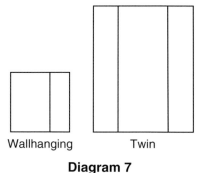

Wallhanging   Twin

Diagram 7

Step 4. For the twin-size quilt, cut the backing fabric into two equal lengths, and trim the selvages. Cut one of the pieces in half lengthwise, and sew one half to each side of the full-width piece, as shown. Press the seams open.

Step 5. Layer the backing, batting, and quilt top, and baste. Quilt as desired.

ADDING THE BINDING

The binding is pieced from short segments of the fabrics used in the rings. Strip piecing is used to speed up the process. You will need four separate binding strips for your quilt.

Step 1. To determine the lengths of the pieced binding strips needed for each side, measure the quilt vertically and add approximately 5 inches, then measure the quilt horizontally and add approximately 5 inches.

Step 2. Sew the 2½-inch-wide strips together lengthwise in any order you find pleasing. Each time you add a strip, sew in the opposite direction from the previous strip to prevent warping. Set each seam by pressing it flat, just as it was sewn, then gently open the strip and press from the right side. Press all seams in the same direction.

Step 3. Using a rotary cutter, trim one end of the strip set, as shown in **Diagram 8**, then cut as many 1¾-inch segments from the strip set as possible.

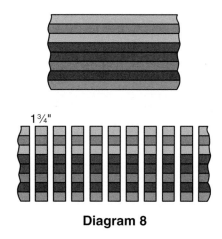

1¾"

Diagram 8

Step 4. Sew the segments together end to end, as shown in **Diagram 9**, constructing two binding strips for each length calculated in Step 1. Make another strip set if necessary, adjusting its width to yield the number of strip units required to complete your binding.

Diagram 9

Step 5. Placing right sides together, match the raw edge of a side binding strip to the raw edge of one side of your quilt, allowing the binding to extend beyond both ends. Sew the binding to the quilt with a $\frac{1}{4}$-inch seam allowance.

Step 6. Turn the binding to the back of the quilt and fold the raw edge under to meet the raw edge of the quilt top. Blindstitch the binding to the quilt backing. Trim excess binding flush with the top and bottom edges of the quilt. Stitch across each end of the binding to help prevent fraying. Repeat for the opposite side of the quilt.

Step 7. Apply the top and bottom binding strips in the same manner, but do not trim the binding flush with the quilt sides. Instead, trim the binding ends so they extend beyond the quilt edge by about $\frac{1}{2}$ inch. Fold under the binding ends before stitching them in place.

FEED SACK WEDDING RING

Skill Level: *Intermediate*

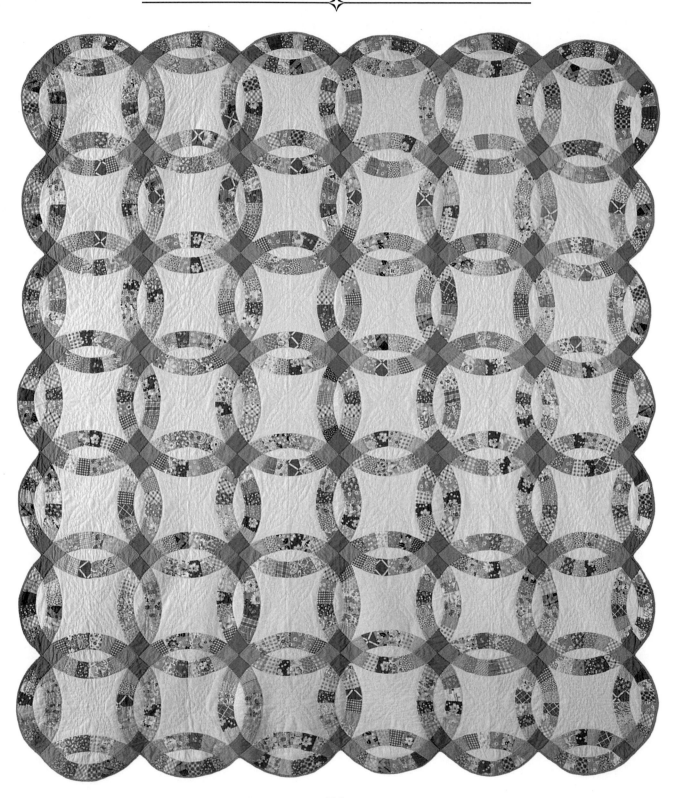

*T*rue to the spirit of the late 1920s, when the Wedding Ring pattern was developed, this delightful example is made from recycled garments and feed sacks. Bertha Rush, the owner of this colorful double-size bed quilt, pointed out that one of her favorite childhood dresses has been preserved in the rings of this quilt. Her grandmother stitched this quilt (along with six others for Bertha's brothers and sisters) in the 1940s, and it was hand quilted by a group of her friends.

BEFORE YOU BEGIN

A large assortment of print fabrics were used to piece the arcs in this traditional quilt, while solid green and pink pieces at their tips complete the rings. In a scrappy quilt like this, color is not as important as variety, so use the yardage requirement for the prints as a guide only—the more prints, the better.

The quilt shown was made primarily with the green-tipped arcs arranged vertically and the pink-tipped arcs arranged horizontally. However, the quiltmaker made a few alterations to this plan along the top row and bottom right corner. To simplify the directions and to avoid the confusion of altering a few of your arcs, we have provided directions that call for all green-tipped arcs to be positioned vertically and all pink-tipped arcs to run horizontally. If you'd like to make your quilt exactly like the quilt in the photograph, you will need 47 green-tipped arc/melon units, 41 pink-tipped arc/melon units, and 9 arc/melon units with one green and one pink tip. Refer to the photograph for the layout.

Quilt Sizes		
	Wallhanging	Double (shown)
Finished Quilt Size	43½" × 43½"	83½" × 96½"
Finished Ring Diameter	18"	18"
Number of Rings	9	42
Number of Pieced Arcs	48	194

Materials		
	Wallhanging	Double
Muslin	1¼ yards	6¾ yards
Assorted prints	1 yard	6 yards
Green solid	¼ yard	¾ yard
Pink solid	¼ yard	¾ yard
Backing	3 yards	7⅝ yards
Batting	50" × 50"	87" × 100"
Binding	½ yard	⅞ yard

NOTE: Yardages are based on 44/45-inch-wide fabrics that are at least 42 inches wide after preshrinking.

CHOOSING FABRICS

Many prints in this Wedding Ring quilt were cut from fabric sacks, a recycling method women used in a more frugal part of this century. Making a replica of this quilt is easy, since an ever-increasing choice of reproduction fabrics is offered at many quilt shops. Period prints are often sold in fat quarters or fat eighths, providing a perfect opportunity to build your scrap collection.

To experiment with other color schemes, photocopy the **Wedding Ring Color Plan** on page 111, and use crayons or colored pencils to create your own design.

75

Cutting Chart

Fabric	Used For	Piece	Number of Pieces	
			Wallhanging	Double
Muslin	Background	A	9	42
	Melons	B	24	97
Assorted prints	Outer wedges of arcs	C	48	194
	Outer wedges of arcs	C reverse	48	194
	Inner wedges of arcs	D	96	776
Green	Connecting wedges	E	24	97
Pink	Connecting wedges	E	24	97

CUTTING

All pattern pieces include ¼-inch seam allowances. Referring to the Cutting Chart, trace and cut the required number of pieces for your quilt size. See page 116 in "Quiltmaking Basics" for information about constructing and using templates.

Note: Cut and piece one sample ring before cutting all of the fabric for the quilt.

PIECING THE ARCS

Step 1. Use chain piecing, an assembly line method that will help speed up the sewing process, to sew pairs of D pieces together. When all of the D pieces have been sewn into pairs, use chain piecing again to link the sewn pairs into units containing four D pieces each, as shown in **Diagram 1.** For more information on chain, or assembly line, piecing, refer to page 117 in "Quiltmaking Basics."

Diagram 1

Step 2. Stack the C and C reverse pieces in separate piles near your sewing machine. Use chain piecing to sew a C piece to the left side of each

Sew Easy

You'll want your rings to have a scrappy look, so mix up the fabrics. Toss all of the D pieces in a bag and shake it up. Then reach in and pull out two pieces and stitch them together. Your quilt will have a scrappier look if you ignore color and value and sew the pieces together as they come out of the bag.

partial arc assembled in Step 1. Next, sew a C reverse piece to the right side of each arc. See **Diagram 2.** Gently press all seams in the same direction, taking care not to stretch the fabric.

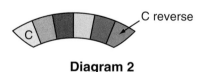

C reverse

Diagram 2

Step 3. Sew a pieced arc to one side of each B melon, as shown in **Diagram 3,** matching the middle seam of the arc with the midpoint of the melon. For more information about piecing curved seams, see page 107 in "Wedding Ring Basics." Press the seam away from the melon. You will use half of the pieced arcs for this step.

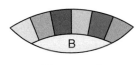

Diagram 3

Step 4. Sew a green E piece to each end of 49 (12 for wallhanging) of the remaining pieced arcs. Press the seams toward the green pieces. Sew the pink E pieces to the remaining 48 (12) arcs. Press the seams away from the pink pieces. See **Diagram 4.**

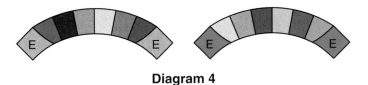

Diagram 4

Step 5. Sew the arcs from Step 4 to the melons, matching the middle seam of the arcs to the mid-point of the melons. Press the seams toward the arcs. You will have two types of arc/melon units— 49 with green tips and 48 with pink tips for the double or 12 each for the wallhanging, as shown in **Diagram 5.**

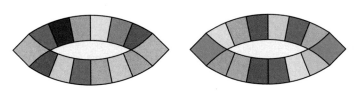

Diagram 5

ASSEMBLING THE QUILT TOP

Step 1. Lay out the completed arc/melon units and background pieces on a design wall or other flat surface.

Important: Note that all arc/melon units with green E pieces are positioned vertically within the quilt top and all arc/melon units with pink E pieces are positioned horizontally.

Step 2. Sew the arc units to the background A pieces in horizontal rows, as shown in the **Partial Assembly Diagram,** leaving ¼ inch open at the beginning and end of each seam and back-stitching. If you are making the wallhanging, your layout will only be three rings wide. Refer to page 109 in "Wedding Ring Basics" for more details about assembling the rings into rows.

Step 3. Sew the rows together, starting and stopping ¼ inch from the end of each arc and backstitching. Press the completed quilt top. Refer to the **Double-Size Quilt Diagram** on page 78 to see all the rows assembled.

QUILTING AND FINISHING

Step 1. Mark the quilt top for quilting. The quilt shown was quilted in the ditch around all the rings, and the background was quilted with a floral motif.

Step 2. Regardless of which quilt size you've chosen to make, the backing will have to be pieced.

Partial Assembly Diagram

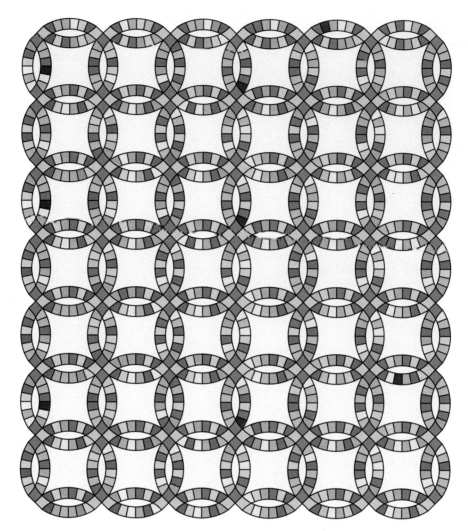

Double-Size Quilt Diagram

For the wallhanging, cut the backing fabric cross-wise into two equal lengths, and trim the selvages. Cut a 36-inch-wide lengthwise panel from one piece and a 16-inch-wide lengthwise panel from the remaining piece. Sew the two panels together, as shown in **Diagram 6.** Press the seam open.

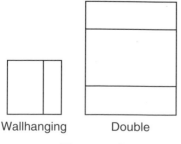

Wallhanging   Double

Diagram 6

Step 3. For the double quilt, cut the backing fabric into three equal lengths, and trim the selvages. Cut a 30-inch-wide panel from two of the segments, then sew one of these panels to each side of the full-width piece, as shown. Press the seams open.

Step 4. Layer the backing, batting, and quilt top, and baste. Quilt as desired.

Step 5. Use a narrow bias binding to bind the quilt, since a narrower binding will be easier to attach around the curves. Refer to the instructions on pages 110 and 121 for information about making bias binding, calculating the amount needed, and applying it around curves.

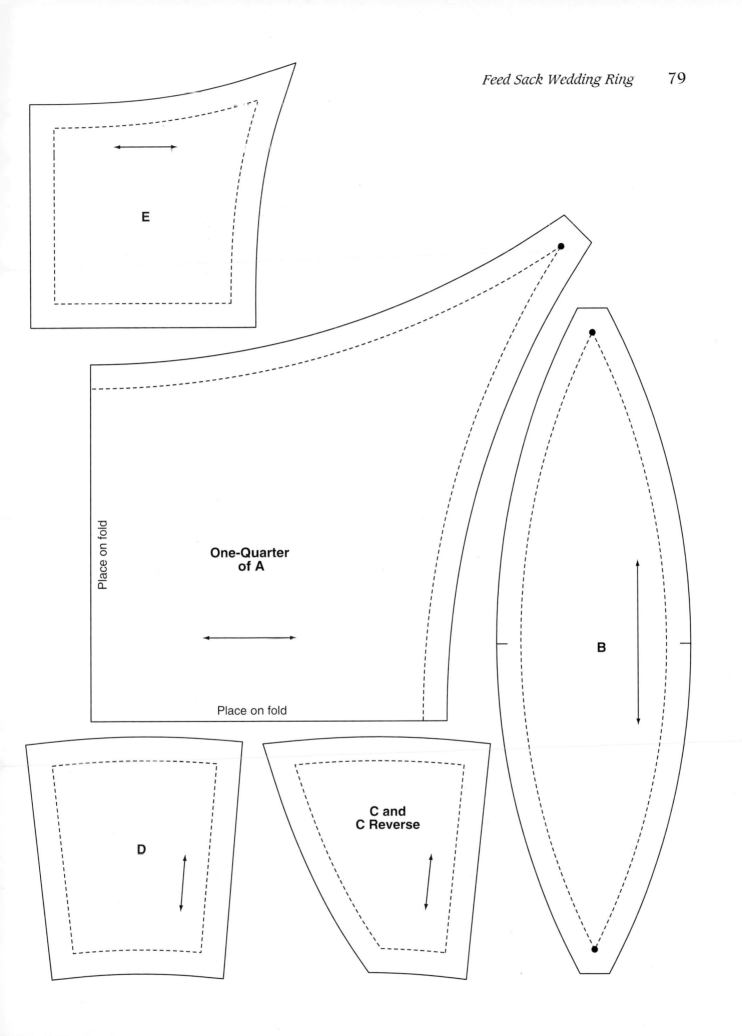

E

Place on fold

One-Quarter of A

Place on fold

B

D

C and C Reverse

PICKLED WATERMELON

Skill Level: *Advanced*

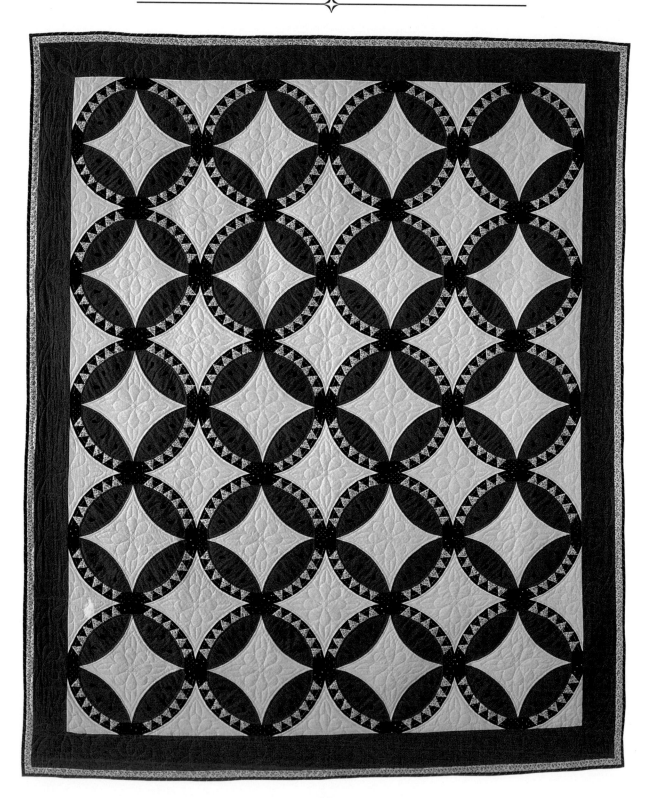

The Pickle Dish is a popular variation of the Wedding Ring quilt, with arcs made of triangles. Julee Prose of Iowa further adapted the pattern to create her unique double-size quilt. In Julee's quilt, the rings are not intertwined as in Double Wedding Ring quilts, and only one side of each melon shape has an arc of triangles. This allows the melon itself to be larger and take on the whimsical look of a watermelon wedge.

BEFORE YOU BEGIN

The arcs of the quilt shown were hand pieced to ensure accuracy of placement of the vine motif in the green print. The directions given here are for machine piecing on paper foundations. The paper gets pulled away from the arcs before they are sewn to the melons.

Paper piecing is fast and fun, and it will give you accurate results. If you aren't familiar with sewing on a foundation, read through the project instructions carefully before beginning. For paper piecing, you will need to trace the C pattern 16 times for the wallhanging or 80 times for the double-size quilt. For a quicker and easier way to prepare your paper foundations, see the "Sew Easy" box on page 83.

In addition to the foundation papers, you will need to make templates for the other pieces in the quilt. Patterns for pieces A, B, C, and D are on pages 87–89. If you prefer to hand piece or machine piece without using foundation papers, you will need to make a template for the triangles and square in the C arc.

Quilt Sizes		
	Wallhanging	Double (shown)
Finished Quilt Size	45½" × 45½"	79½" × 96½"
Finished Ring Diameter	17"	17"
Number of Rings	4	20
Number of Pieced Arcs	16	80

Materials		
	Wallhanging	Double
White-on-white print	2⅛ yards	9⅝ yards
Rose print	1½ yards	4½ yards
White-and-rose print	¾ yard	2½ yards
Green print	½ yard	2 yards
Assorted dark green prints	¼ yard	⅞ yard
Black solid	⅛ yard	¼ yard
Backing	3⅛ yards	7½ yards
Batting	53" × 53"	87" × 104"
Binding	½ yard	¾ yard

NOTE: Yardages are based on 44/45-inch-wide fabrics that are at least 42 inches wide after preshrinking.

This quilt is assembled with complete background A pieces, as well as with half-A and quarter-A pieces. Folding the A pattern piece, which is given as one-quarter of its full size, along the two straight edges will yield a full-size A template. To make templates for the half-A and quarter-A pieces that will go around the outer edges of the quilt, you will need to adapt the A pattern piece slightly.

To make a half-A template,

81

Cutting Chart

Fabric	Used For	Piece	Number of Pieces	
			Wallhanging	Double
White-on-white print	Background	A	5	32
	Background	Half-A	4	14
	Background	Quarter-A	4	4
Rose print	Melons	B	16	80
Black	Seeds	D	48	240

Fabric	Used For	Strip Width	Number of Strips	
			Wallhanging	Double
White-and-rose print	Arcs	2¼"	1 to start	1 to start
	Outer border	1½"	5	9
Green print	Arcs	2¼"	1 to start	1 to start
Assorted dark greens	Arcs	2¼"	1 to start	1 to start
Rose print	Inner border	5"	5	9

trace the pattern once, then flip it along one fold line and trace again. You then need to add a ¼-inch seam allowance along the long straight edge before cutting. To make the quarter-A template, trace the pattern as shown, then add a ¼-inch seam allowance along both straight edges before cutting.

For information on making and using templates, see page 116 in "Quiltmaking Basics."

CHOOSING FABRICS

The quiltmaker chose fabrics to enhance the watermelon theme. Rosy pink melons are dotted with black seeds and surrounded by green and white triangle rinds. All triangles in the pieced arcs repeat the same two prints. The squares at the ends of the arcs are sewn from an assortment of four dark green prints that closely match each other in color and value. Although the quiltmaker used a vine-striped fabric for her green rinds, we suggest that you avoid using fabrics with direc-

tional prints with the paper-piecing method.

If you prefer to use a directional print, we recommend that you make traditional see-through templates from the shapes in the C arc. You can then lay the templates over the fabric as you trace and cut to make sure your directional print is placed correctly. With this method, you would be more successful with hand piecing than with machine piecing.

To make pickled watermelons, you'll probably want to select similar colors to those used in the quilt shown. However, if you would like a completely different look, photocopy the **Wedding Ring Color Plan** on page 111 and use colored pencils or crayons to create a color scheme that is uniquely yours.

CUTTING

All measurements include ¼-inch seam allowances. Referring to the Cutting Chart, cut the required number of pieces for your quilt size. For the foundation piecing technique, cut individual pieces from the strips as you go along. We recommend cutting only one strip of each fabric to start, as you may find that you would like a slightly wider or narrower strip to work with.

Note: Cut and piece one sample ring before cutting all of the fabric for the quilt.

PIECING THE ARCS

The arcs are pieced on paper foundations. With this method, an entire arc, represented by pattern piece C, is drawn full size on paper. The only seam allowance included is the one around the outer perimeter of the pattern piece. You will stitch your pieces directly to the paper, then remove the paper before sewing the arcs to the melon unit.

— Sew Easy —

You can trace templates with a hot-iron transfer pen or pencil, then use a medium-hot iron to transfer the image to paper foundations. You can usually get five or six prints from each tracing. Blank newsprint is a good choice for foundation piecing since it is sturdy enough to remain intact while you sew yet easy to tear away when you are finished with the quilt. Pads of newsprint in a variety of sizes are usually available at office- or school-supply stores.

Step 1. Template C consists of two halves—the left half and the right half. Trace one of each, then connect the halves, matching the dots. You will need one complete arc foundation for each pieced arc used in your quilt. If you have access to a photocopier that will make exact duplicates, it can be used to make copies. Trace the image as close to the center of your page as possible to help eliminate the distortion that sometimes takes place around the outer edges of photocopies. Make sure the page is perfectly flat against the

······ Sew Quick ······

Layer several sheets of tracing paper beneath your original tracing. Slip the stack under your sewing machine needle, and carefully stitch on all traced lines without thread in your machine. The punched holes are easy to see from either side of the tracing paper, and the additional perforations make the paper especially easy to tear away later. You can stitch about eight to ten sheets at a time.

copier's glass before beginning. Always compare copied images to the original templates before using them.

If you don't have access to a photocopier, trace each template individually. Use a fine-tip pen or a pencil sharpened often to keep lines narrow and uniform. This will help to ensure consistent seam lines and accurate piecing. This is the least desirable transfer method, however, since variations are more likely to occur when you make a large number of hand-drawn copies. See the "Sew Easy" and "Sew Quick" boxes for other transfer methods.

Step 2. Position a 2¼-inch strip of assorted dark green fabrics right side up at one end of the back side of the foundation, as shown in **Diagram 1**.

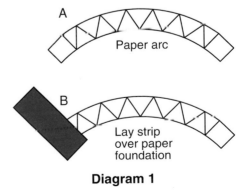

Diagram 1

Be sure that the fabric completely covers the end square on the pattern and that it also extends approximately ¼ inch past the line separating the square from the first triangle. If you are new to foundation piecing, you may find it easier at first to pin your first fabric in place. Do not sew yet.

Step 3. Position a 2¼-inch strip of assorted dark green fabric for the first triangle right side down on the foundation, as shown in **Diagram 2**, matching edges with the first dark green fabric where it overlaps the stitching line separating the two pieces. Hold or pin the two fabrics in place, flip the foundation over, and stitch directly on the line separating the square from the first triangle. Use a slightly shorter than normal stitch length, and begin and end the seam a few stitches past the drawn line.

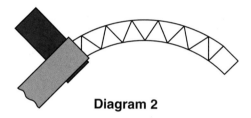

Diagram 2

Step 4. Turn to the reverse of the foundation and flip the second green strip right side up. Trim the seam allowance a bit if necessary to reduce bulk. Finger press the piece in place, or press with a warm iron. Cut away the excess tails from your fabric strips, but be sure to leave enough fabric to overlap the outer edges of the template. You must also leave enough of the second strip so that approximately ¼ inch of fabric overlaps all points of the line between the first and second triangles.

Step 5. Position a 2¼-inch white-and-rose print strip right side down on the foundation, as shown in **Diagram 3**. Holding the fabric in place, flip the foundation over, and sew along the line separating the first triangle from the second. Remove the foundation from your sewing machine, flip the foundation over, trim the seam allowance to a scant ¼ inch, and finger press. Continue adding green and white-and-rose pieces in the same manner until you have completed the arc.

Don't get confused about which direction your

fabric should be facing. The first piece of fabric is the *only* one placed right side up. All other pieces are positioned right side down for sewing. Also, remember that all fabric gets positioned on the back of the foundation paper, but all sewing takes place on the top, or right side, of the paper.

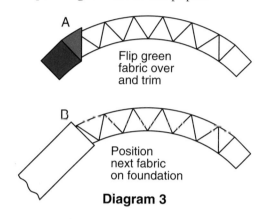

Diagram 3

Step 6. When all pieces have been sewn to the foundation, press with a warm iron. Using scissors or rotary-cutting equipment, cut on the outermost line of the foundation. Tear away the paper, taking care not to stretch the fabric.

Step 7. Repeat Steps 2 through 6 to construct the remaining pieced arcs required for your quilt.

— Sew Easy —

Paper piecing is a lot easier if you roughly trace the pattern from the right side of the paper to the back side. You will be stitching from the exact lines on the right side but positioning your fabrics from the wrong side. A rough tracing will help you align your fabrics so you won't come up short in the seam allowances. A light box or window is a big help for easier tracing.

ASSEMBLING THE RINGS

Step 1. Matching centers, sew a rose print B melon to each pieced arc, as shown in **Diagram 4**.

Press the seams toward the melons. Refer to page 107 in "Wedding Ring Basics" for more information about sewing curved seams.

Diagram 4

Step 2. Sew four melon/arc units to each full-size white-on-white background A piece, as shown in **Diagram 5**. Press the seams toward the melons. Again, refer to page 107 in "Wedding Ring Basics" if you need more details on assembling these pieces. You will have leftover A pieces, which will be used to assemble the quilt top.

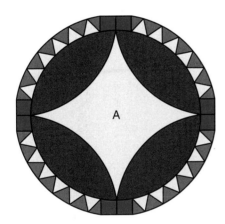

Diagram 5

ASSEMBLING THE QUILT TOP

Step 1. Using a design wall or other flat surface, lay out the completed rings in horizontal rows, along with the half-A and quarter-A pieces, as shown in the **Partial Assembly Diagram**.

Step 2. Beginning with the top row, connect the white background pieces to the first row of rings. Add the next row of background pieces, then the next row of rings. Continue sewing rows together until the quilt top is assembled. Press all seams away from the white background pieces.

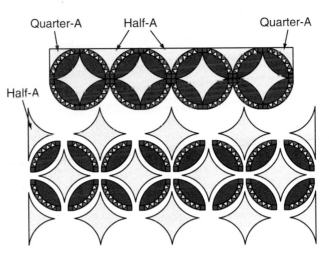

Partial Assembly Diagram

Remember to start and stop each seam ¼ inch from the ends of the white background pieces. Refer to page 107 for additional information about sewing curved seams.

Step 3. Using the appliqué technique of your choice, stitch three black seeds to each rose melon. Refer to the photograph on page 80 for placement. For information about one appliqué technique, refer to page 118.

ADDING THE MITERED BORDERS

The inner rose and outer white-and-rose print borders will be joined together first, then the two will be sewn to the quilt top as one unit.

Step 1. To determine the length of the side borders, measure the quilt top vertically through the center. To this measurement, add two times the finished width of the inner and outer borders (5½ inches × 2) plus approximately 5 inches. This is the length you need for each side border. In the same manner, measure the quilt top horizontally through the center, and calculate the length of the top and bottom borders.

Step 2. Sew the rose border strips together end to end to make a top, bottom, and two side borders in the sizes you've calculated. Sew the white-and-rose outer border strips together in the same

Double-Size Quilt Diagram

manner. Be sure to keep the side border strips separate from the top and bottom border strips.

Step 3. Pin and sew the rose border strips to the corresponding white-and-rose print strips. Press the seams toward the rose borders.

Step 4. Pin and sew the four borders to the quilt top, with the wide rose border on the inside. Refer to page 119 in "Quiltmaking Basics" for instructions on adding borders with mitered corners.

When preparing the miters, be sure to carefully match the two strips in adjacent borders. See the **Double-Size Quilt Diagram.**

Quilting and Finishing

Step 1. Mark the quilt top for quilting. The quilt shown has a floral motif in the center of each ring and in the borders. Outline quilting highlights the rings.

Step 2. Regardless of which quilt size you've chosen to make, the backing will have to be pieced. To make the backing for the wallhanging, cut the backing fabric crosswise into two equal lengths, and trim the selvages. From one length, cut a 13-inch-wide panel. Sew this narrow panel to one side of the full-width panel, as shown in **Diagram 6.** Press the seam open.

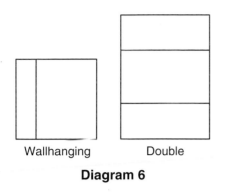

Wallhanging   Double

Diagram 6

Step 3. For the double-size quilt, cut the backing fabric crosswise into three equal lengths, and trim the selvages. Cut a 32-inch-wide panel from two of the segments, then sew one of these to each side of the full-width piece, as shown. Press the seams open.

Step 4. Layer the backing, batting, and quilt top, and baste. Quilt as desired.

Step 5. Make and attach double-fold binding, referring to the directions on page 121 in "Quiltmaking Basics" for information. To calculate the amount of binding needed for your quilt size, add the length of the four sides of the quilt plus 9 inches. The total is the approximate number of inches of binding you will need.

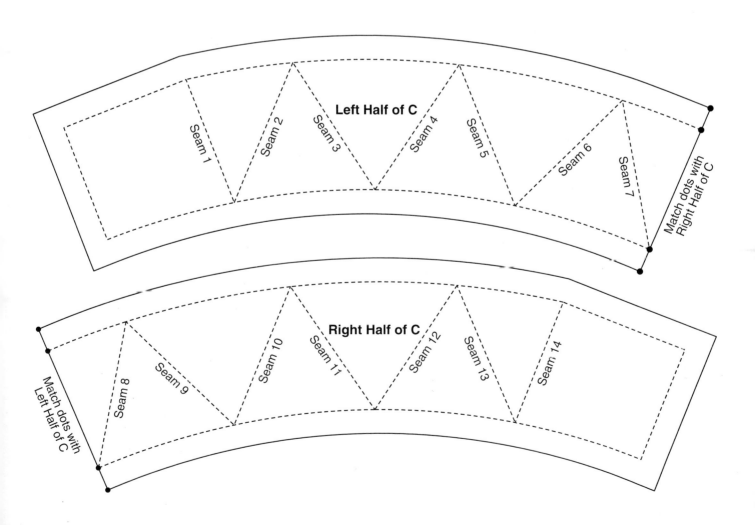

Fold

One-Quarter of A

Fold

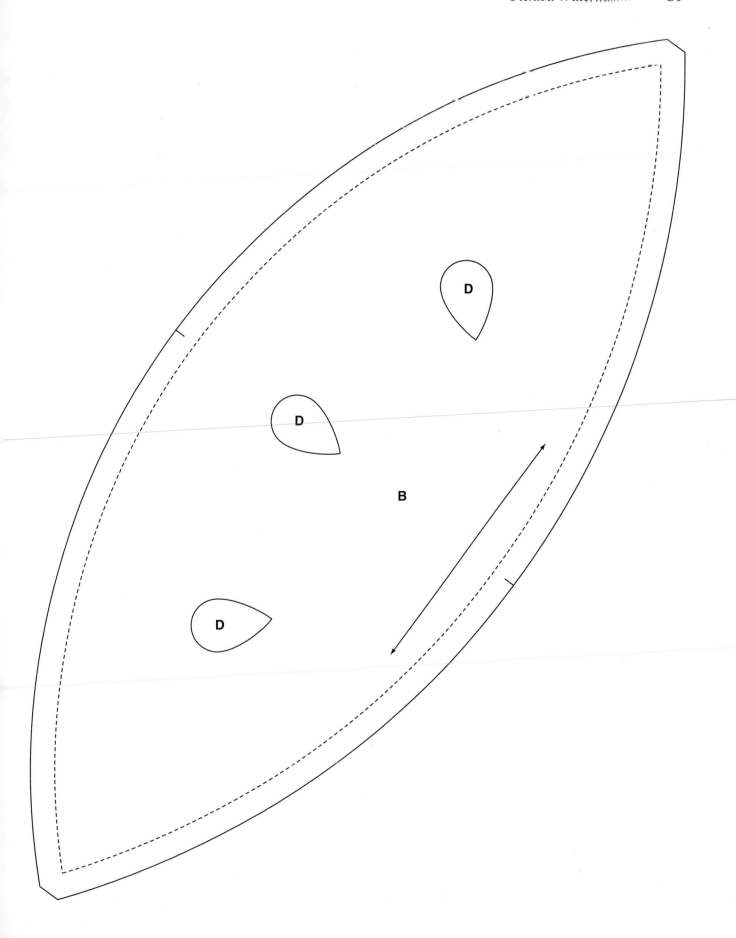

SILVER ANNIVERSARY

Skill Level: *Challenging*

Designed by Annie Segal for the twenty-fifth anniversary issue of Quilter's Newsletter Magazine, *this dazzling queen-size quilt would be a spectacular addition to any bed. Paper foundation piecing methods are used for accuracy among all the intersecting triangle seams in the arcs and stars of this intricate quilt. While we don't recommend this quilt for the fainthearted, it is a dazzling beauty that is sure to become your best quilt if you are up to the challenge.*

BEFORE YOU BEGIN

This Double Wedding Ring quilt looks quite intricate, but an accurate, simplified assembly can be achieved by using paper foundations to piece the arcs and little stars. In addition, you will need to make templates for pattern pieces A through P on pages 98–103. Notice that some of the patterns are overlapped, so pay close attention to the cutting lines for each pattern. For information on making and using templates, see page 116 in "Quiltmaking Basics."

We recommend that you read the project instructions carefully before beginning to be sure you understand all the quilt's components and the methods used.

CHOOSING FABRICS

The quilt contains several different pink, rose, orchid, and purple fabrics. To eliminate confusion later, label a sample of each fabric with its name. You may also find it helpful to label each cut strip and jot down identifying names onto paper foundations.

We suggest you choose fabrics that do not have a directional print. The pieces are turned every

Quilt Size

Finished Quilt Size	100" × 100"
Finished Ring Size	16¼"
Number of Rings	29
Number of Pieced Arcs	116
Number of Pieced Stars	60

NOTE: *Due to the complexity of the design, no size variations are provided.*

Materials

	Amount
Cream	6⅛ yards
Silver print	4 yards
Light rose	⅜ yard
Medium rose	½ yard
Medium pink	¾ yard
Bright pink	1⅛ yards
Wine	½ yard
Light purple	½ yard
Medium purple	¾ yard
Dark purple	1 yard
Very dark purple	1½ yards
Light gray solid	⅜ yard
Orchid	4½ yards
Backing	9⅛ yards
Batting	108" × 108"
Binding	¾ yard

NOTE: *Yardages are based on 44/45-inch-wide fabrics that are at least 42 inches wide after preshrinking.*

91

Cutting Chart

Fabric	Used For	Strip Width	Number of Strips
Cream	Stars	4"	16
	Arcs	3¼"	12
Silver print	Stars	3½"	12
Light rose	Arcs	3¼"	3
Medium rose	Arcs	3¼"	4
Medium pink	Stars	3"	8
Bright pink	Stars	3"	12
Wine	Stars	3"	5
Light purple	Arcs	3¼"	4
Medium purple	Arcs	3¼"	7
Dark purple	Arcs	3¼"	9
Very dark purple	Stars	4"	3
	Arcs	3¼"	4
Light gray solid	Middle border	1"	10
Orchid	Arcs	3¼"	5
	Outer border	10"	10

Fabric	Used For	Number of Pieces
Cream	Background	9 A, 8 C, 4 D, 24 E, 28 G, 4 H, 4 H reverse, 8 I, 4 J, 40 K
Silver print	Background	4 A, 8 B, 4 C, 4 D, 20 E, 28 F
Very dark purple	Inner border	16 L, 8 M

which way in the quilt, so a directional print may be distracting. Our instructions refer to the colors used in the original quilt. Use the **Wedding Ring Color Plan** on page 111 to devise your own color scheme if you like. Then, before you cut or sew, substitute the fabrics you'll be using for the colors given in the instructions. For example, if you select a range of blue fabrics, mark each fabric so you'll remember if it's to be used in place of the rose, orchid, or pink fabric shown in the diagrams.

CUTTING

All measurements include ¼-inch seam allowances. Referring to the Cutting Chart, cut the required number of strips for the stars and arcs (foundation piecing sections N, O, and P) as well as for the borders. Then cut the required number of pieces using templates A through M. The strips used for piecing the stars and arcs will be trimmed as you go. There is no need to cut the strips into smaller pieces before you start stitching.

Note: Cut and piece one sample ring before cutting all of the fabric for the quilt.

UNDERSTANDING THE QUILT COMPONENTS

It's important to understand all of the quilt's design elements and how they will be used to assemble the quilt top. As you read this section, refer to the photograph on page 90 and the

Assembly Diagram on page 97 for an overall view of the different components and their affect on the quilt design,

Stars

Unit 1 stars, as shown in **Diagram 1A,** are used in the central portion of the quilt. Unit 2 stars, as shown in **1B,** are nearly identical; the only difference is that one corner is unattached. This corner is sewn into the border, giving Unit 2 stars a three-dimensional effect. **Diagram 2** illustrates the three color variations needed for each type of star. These stars will be pieced on paper foundations.

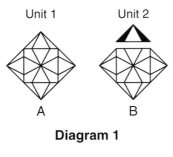

Diagram 1

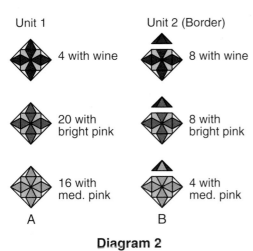

Diagram 2

Arcs

Units 3 and 4 are foundation pieced arcs. The color and value schemes used for the arcs are illustrated in **Diagram 3.** Notice that the contrast between colors in the Unit 3 arcs is much greater than that in the Unit 4 arcs. The Unit 3 arcs are used in the center rings of the quilt, while the Unit 4 arcs are used in the outer rings.

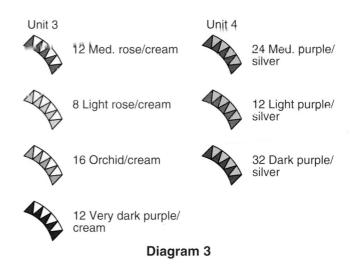

Diagram 3

Template Pieces

Templates A through M are used to cut individual pieces. **Diagram 4** shows how many of each template to cut from each color. Refer to the **Assembly Diagram** for their position in the quilt.

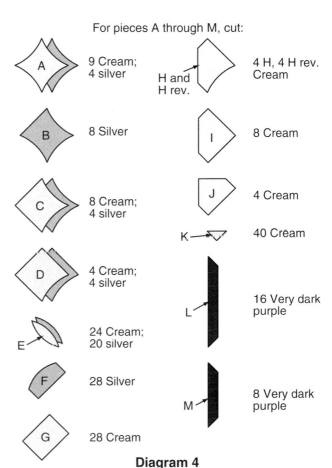

Diagram 4

PIECING UNIT 1 STARS

If you haven't tried foundation piecing, you're in for a treat. With this method, an entire block, or in this case a portion of a block, is drawn to scale on paper or another foundation material. The only seam allowance included is the one around the outer perimeter of the block.

The fabric is positioned on the reverse side of the foundation. All sewing takes place on the front of the foundation, directly on drawn seam lines. If you are unfamiliar with this technique, it may at first seem awkward. But if you position the fabric correctly and are careful to sew on the lines, every piece in the block will be perfect.

Step 1. Two N foundations and four O foundations are used to assemble each of the 60 star units. Make 120 exact copies of N and 240 copies of O. If you have access to a photocopier that will make exact duplicates, trace multiple copies of the two templates onto a sheet of paper, including the numbers that indicate the piecing order, then copy them. Trace the images as near to the center of your page as possible to help eliminate the distortion that sometimes takes place around the outer edges of copies.

Also make sure the page is perfectly flat against the copier's glass before beginning. Always compare copied images to the original templates before using them. For alternate methods of making paper foundations, see the "Sew Easy" and "Sew Quick" boxes on page 83.

Step 2. To piece the Unit 1 stars, you will use the following strips: the 3-inch-wide wine, bright pink, and medium pink; the 3½-inch-wide silver; and the 4-inch-wide cream. When foundation piecing, pieces are sewn in numerical order following the order on each foundation. Begin with an N foundation paper. Position one end of a wine strip right side up on the back side of the foundation. The fabric should completely cover the first section. Be sure the fabric extends at least ¼ inch past the line separating piece 1 from piece 2 and that it overlaps the outer perimeter of the seam allowance, as shown in **Diagram 5.** (If the lines aren't visible through your paper, hold the foundation and the positioned fabric up to the light to check.)

Diagram 5

Step 3. Next, place a silver strip right side down on top of the wine strip, matching edges where the wine fabric overlaps the line separating pieces 1 and 2, as shown in **Diagram 6.** Holding the two fabrics in place, flip the foundation over and stitch on that line, as shown in **Diagram 7.** For stability, begin and end your seam approximately ⅛ inch beyond each end of the line.

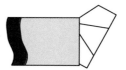

Diagram 6

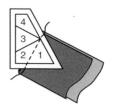

Diagram 7

········ Sew Quick········

Trace two N templates and four O templates—the number needed for one star block—on a single sheet of paper. Make 60 photocopies. With each full block on a page, you can easily make notations that may be helpful later, such as jotting down the color code to be used for individual pieces.

Step 4. Turn again to the back side of your foundation. If it's too bulky, trim the seam allowance between the two pieces you've just sewn, then flip the silver strip right side up and finger press it in place. Trim away the long ends of both strips, leaving enough fabric on each to extend past the ¼-inch seam allowances. Make sure at least ¼ inch of silver fabric extends beyond the next seam line—the line separating pieces 2 and 3. It's better to allow extra rather than skimp on the seam allowance.

Step 5. The third piece is sewn in exactly the same manner. Place a wine strip right side down along the edge of piece 2 where it overlaps the line between pieces 2 and 3. Sew, trim the seam if necessary, flip the fabric over, and finger press. Repeat the same steps with silver fabric for piece 4.

Step 6. Press the block lightly with a warm iron. Using a rotary cutter and ruler, trim away excess fabric by cutting exactly on the outermost line of the foundation. This automatically creates a ¼-inch seam allowance around your block segment.

Step 7. Make a second N foundation block in exactly the same manner. Sew the two N pieces together, as shown in **Diagram 8**.

Diagram 8

Step 8. Make four star points using four O foundations. Refer to **Diagram 2** on page 93 for color requirements. Assemble the O sections in exactly the same manner as you did the N sections, sewing the pieces in numerical order.

Step 9. Sew the four completed O sections to the partially assembled star, as shown in **Diagram 9**.

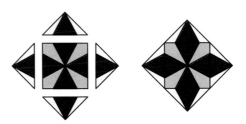

Diagram 9

Step 10. Repeat Steps 2 through 9 to assemble the remaining 39 Unit 1 stars, referring to **Diagram 2** for color requirements.

PIECING UNIT 2 STARS

Unit 2 stars use the same color and size fabric strips as for Unit 1 stars, plus the 4-inch-wide very dark purple strips.

Step 1. Unit 2 stars are pieced in the same manner as Unit 1 stars, except that one O section for each star is assembled with very dark purple for pieces 2 and 3. Make 40 N sections and 80 O sections, referring to **Diagram 2** on page 93 for color requirements.

Step 2. When assembling the Unit 2 star sections into a block, sew all sections together as you did for the Unit 1 stars, except for the O section with the very dark purple fabric. Set this corner aside. It will be sewn into the inner purple border when the quilt is assembled.

— Sew Easy —

Leave the paper foundations for the N and O sections of the Unit 1 and Unit 2 stars in place until the quilt top is assembled. This will keep all block edges straight and square until you are ready to stitch them together. To reduce bulk, you may want to remove the paper along the seam allowances where star segments meet.

PIECING UNIT 3 AND 4 ARCS

Step 1. Make a total of 116 arc foundation papers from Template P, following the method you used to make foundations N and O.

Step 2. Referring to **Diagram 3** on page 93 for color requirements, begin with piece 1 and use the same method to assemble the arcs that was used to assemble the stars. When each entire foundation has been pieced, use scissors to trim the excess fabric around the perimeter. For ease in piecing the curves, remove the paper foundations from the arcs before they are stitched into the quilt.

ASSEMBLING THE QUILT TOP

The quilt is assembled in diagonal rows, then the rows are joined, as shown in the **Assembly Diagram.** Use a flat surface or design wall to lay out your blocks and background pieces, as shown.

When possible, press seams in adjoining rows in opposite directions. Be as accurate as possible with your ¼-inch seam allowances to help ensure that star points in the pieced border will match up correctly with the Unit 2 stars in the quilt top. The instructions that follow may help you sort the pieces, but refer to the illustrations for a visual guide.

Background pieces: The nine center rings have cream backgrounds, while the surrounding set of rings have silver backgrounds. The outermost background pieces are cream.

Unit 1 stars: The four wine Unit 1 stars are around the very center ring of the quilt. Twelve bright pink Unit 1 stars connect the rings that surround the center ring. The 16 medium pink Unit 1 stars are added next. Two bright pink Unit 1 stars complete each corner ring.

Unit 2 stars: These stars all touch the dark purple inner border. A medium pink Unit 2 star is at the midpoint of each side of the quilt, with a bright pink Unit 2 star to either side of it. The wine Unit 2 stars are positioned diagonally from each other near the corners of the quilt top.

Arcs: Unit 3 arcs are used in the center of the quilt. Unit 4 arcs are around the outer sections of the quilt. Notice that in some rows, the arcs must be joined with an E or F piece before a diagonal row can be sewn. Refer to page 107 in "Wedding Ring Basics" for instructions on piecing curved seams.

MAKING THE BORDERS

Pieced Inner Border

Sew together four border strips, as shown in the **Assembly Diagram.** Each border begins and ends with a very dark purple M piece as shown, and five Unit 2 stars alternate with four very dark purple L pieces in between. Be sure to position the star corners so their colors correspond with like colors in the quilt top. Fold each border in half crosswise to find its center, then crease it.

Gray Middle Border

Sew two-and-one-half light gray strips together end to end to make one border strip. Trim the border to 84 inches long. Repeat to make four

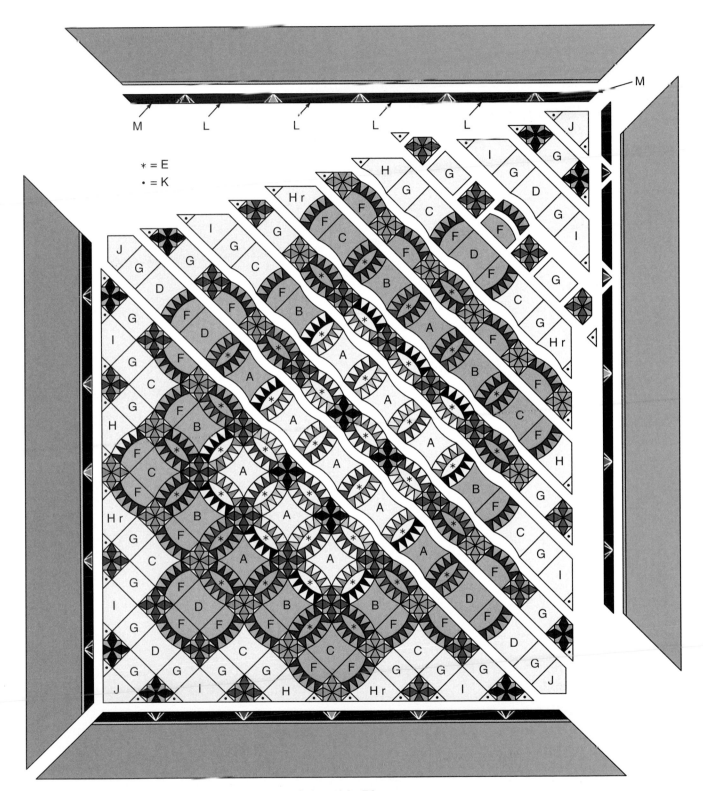

Assembly Diagram

such borders. With wrong sides together, fold each strip in half *lengthwise* and press. Fold cross-wise to find its center. Set aside.

Orchid Outer Border

Sew two-and-one-half orchid strips together end to end to make one border strip. Trim the border to 102½ inches long. Repeat to make four such borders. Fold each border crosswise to find its center.

ADDING THE BORDERS

Step 1. Place a pieced border and an orchid border right sides together, sandwiching a folded light gray middle border between them. Match the centers and raw edges on all three borders. Pin at the center and along the raw edges. Sew the borders together. Repeat with the borders for the remaining three sides of the quilt.

Step 2. Press each gray strip toward the orchid border. Press the seam allowances toward the pieced border.

Step 3. Sew a border unit to each side of the quilt, carefully aligning the Unit 2 star corners in the border with their counterparts at the edge of the quilt. Miter the corners of the borders, referring to page 119 in "Quiltmaking Basics" for more information.

Step 4. Remove all remaining paper foundations from the quilt top.

QUILTING AND FINISHING

Step 1. Mark the quilt top for quilting. The quilt shown was machine quilted with a combina-

tion of in-the-ditch quilting around the rings, star motif quilting in the centers of the rings, and additional circles and stars in the cream background and orchid border. The star quilting motif is given on the A/B/C/D pattern.

Step 2. The backing for this quilt will have to be pieced. Cut the backing fabric crosswise into three equal lengths, each 105 inches, and trim the selvages. Trim each length to 36 inches wide, and sew the panels together lengthwise, as shown in **Diagram 10.** Press the seams open.

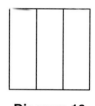

Diagram 10

Step 3. Layer the quilt top, batting, and backing, and baste the layers together. Quilt as desired.

Step 4. Referring to the directions on page 121 in "Quiltmaking Basics," make and attach double-fold binding. To calculate the amount of binding needed, add the length of the four sides of the quilt plus 9 inches. The total is the approximate number of inches of binding you will need for your quilt.

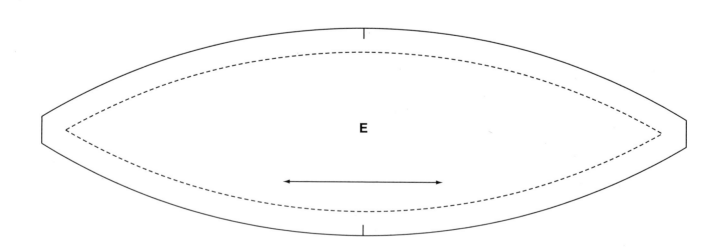

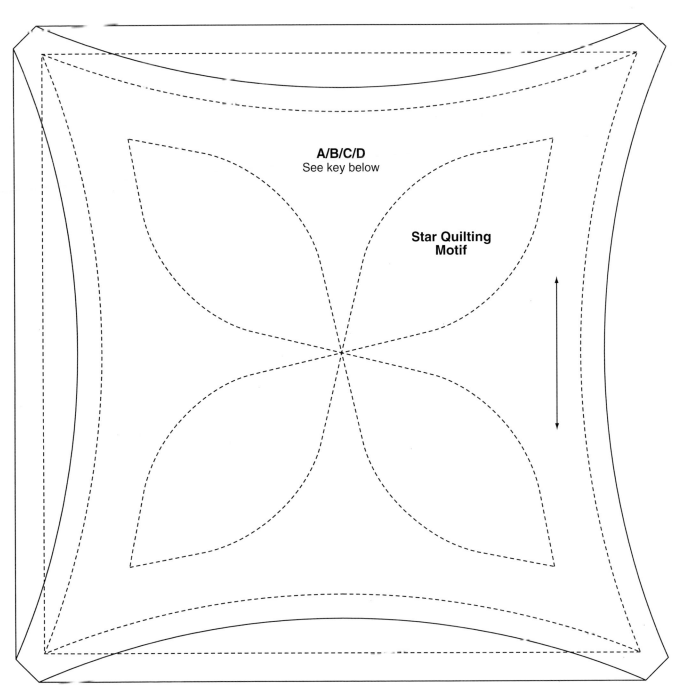

A/B/C/D
See key below

**Star Quilting
Motif**

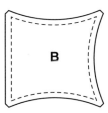

A

Cut template
A with four
curved sides

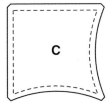

B

Cut template
B with three
curved sides

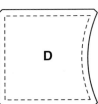

C

Cut template
C with two
curved sides

D

Cut template
D with one
curved side

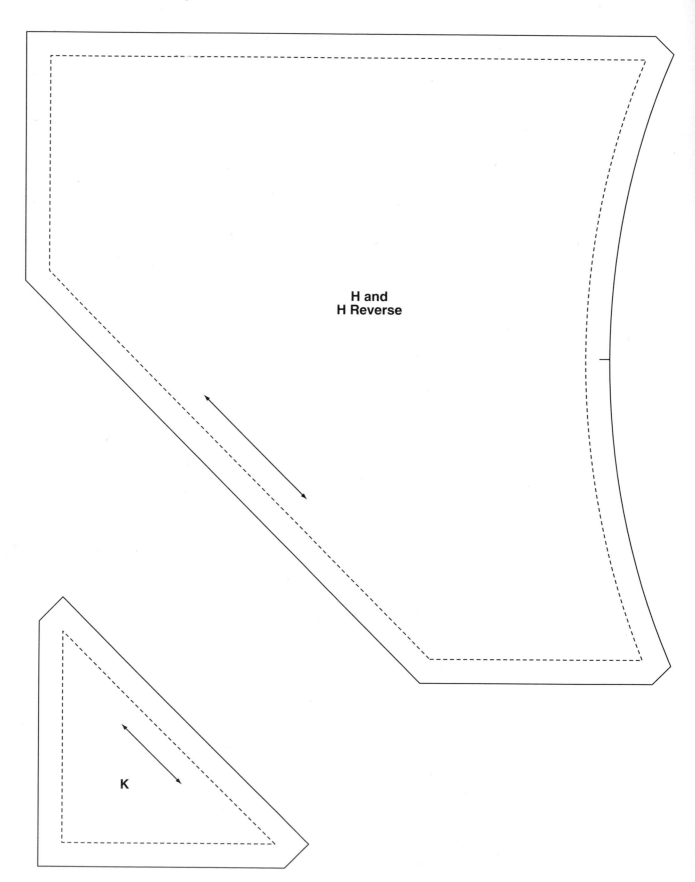

**H and
H Reverse**

K

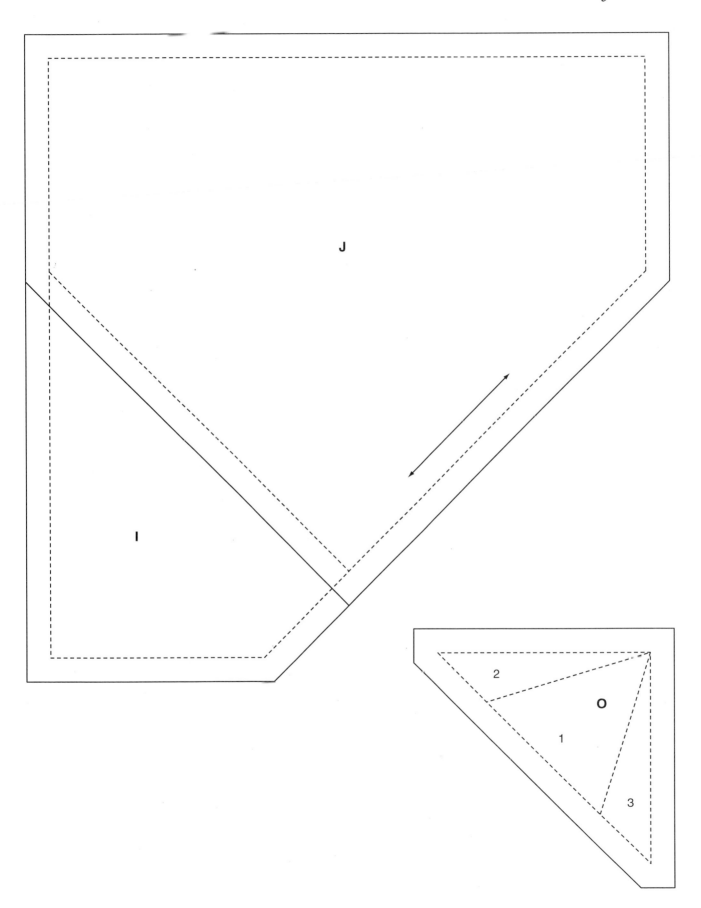

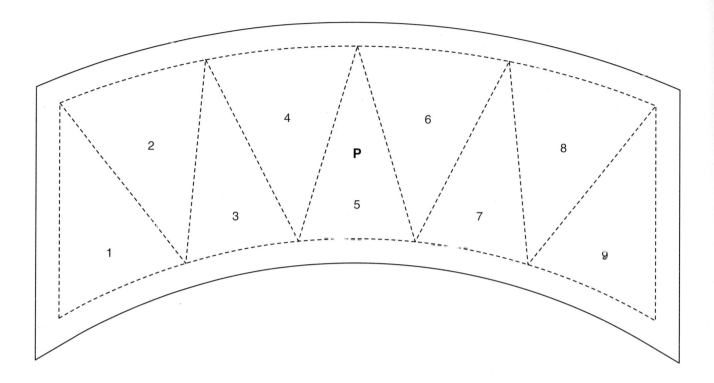

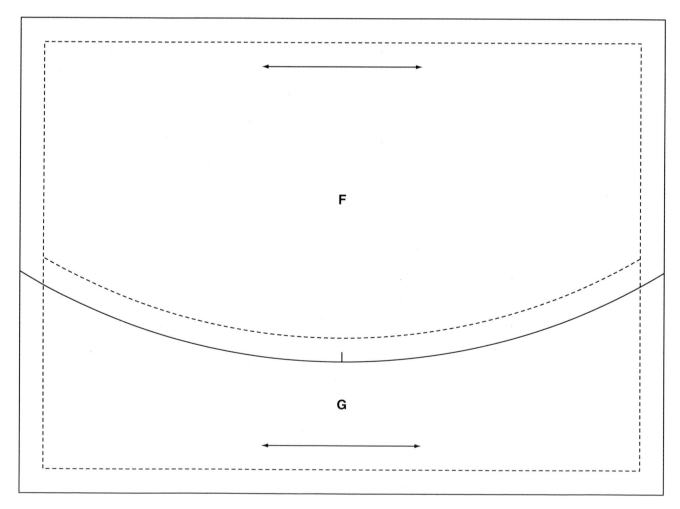

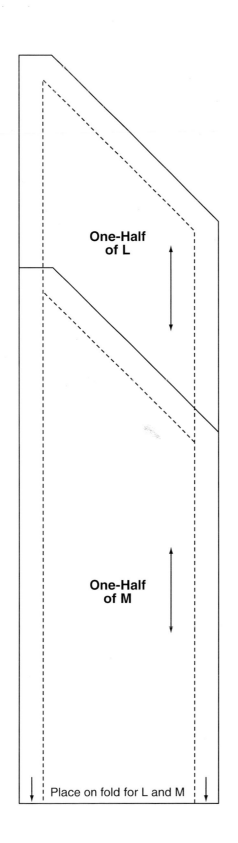

**One-Half
of L**

**One-Half
of M**

Place on fold for L and M

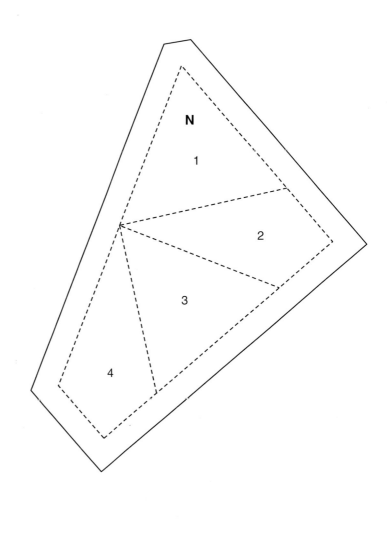

N

1

2

3

4

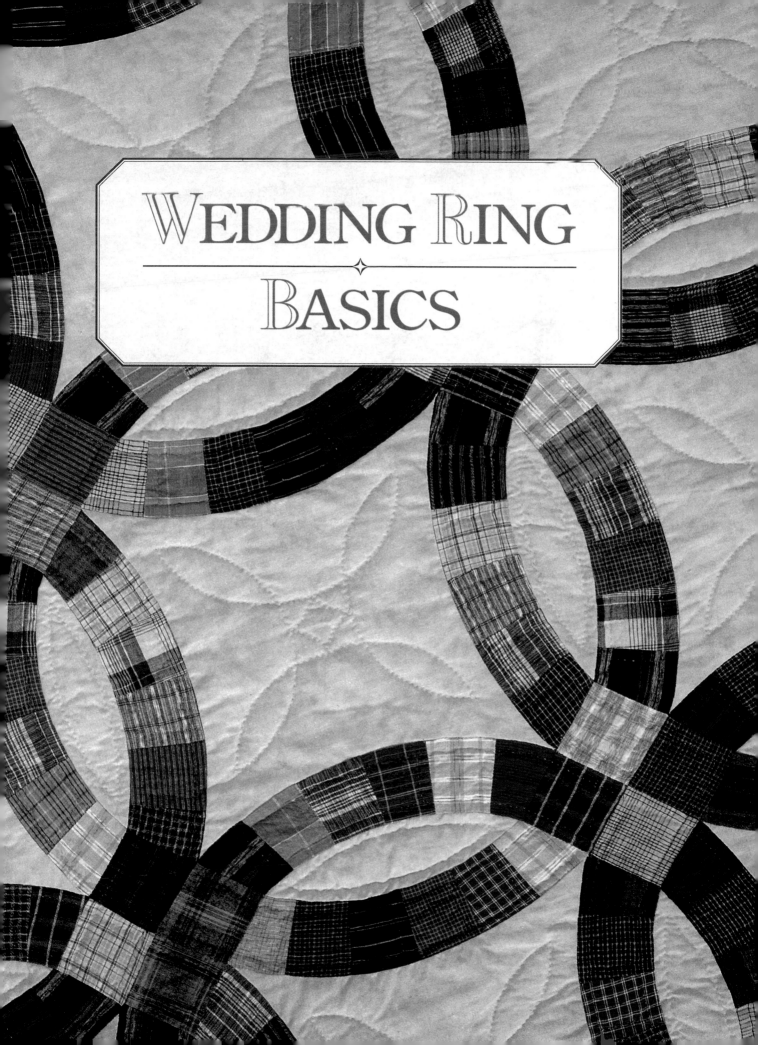

WEDDING RING
BASICS

WEDDING RING COMPONENTS

Most traditional double wedding ring quilts have similar components and are cut and sewn in much the same way. A complete ring typically consists of a center background and four pieced oval segments. An oval segment is comprised of two pieced arcs stitched to opposite sides of a melon, with connecting wedges at each end. **Diagram 1** shows the parts of a ring and how they look when sewn together.

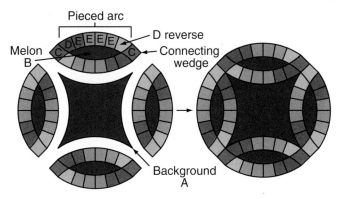

Diagram 1

Some wedding ring quilts have solid arcs, such as Job's Tears and Heart and Hand. The solid arcs are often connected with the same type of wedges as pieced arcs. In this book, however, the solid arc quilts are connected with pentagons and Nine-Patch blocks for an interesting twist on tradition.

Complete rings are not usually sewn together side by side. Instead, the oval segments are shared with neighboring rings, as shown in **Diagram 2**, to create the intertwining design we are so familiar with.

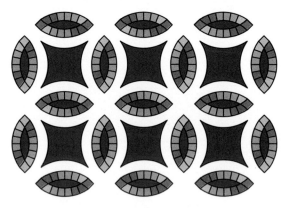

Diagram 2

PLANNING YOUR COLOR SCHEME

To help you create your own color plan for any of the quilts in this book, photocopy the **Wedding Ring Color Plan** on page 111, and use crayons or colored pencils to experiment with different color schemes. While each project in this book is unique, there are some similarities about the way Wedding Ring quilts and their variations are assembled, so a traditional Double Wedding Ring quilt pattern is used for the color plan. With a little imagination or perhaps a few lines drawn by you, you can customize the color plan to help you visualize your project and the colors and fabrics of your preference.

Sew Easy

If you don't have access to hand-dyed fabrics in your local quilt shop, several companies offer them by mail. Several also have swatch cards available.

Alaska Dyeworks
   (907) 373-6562
   Mottled, progressions, color wheels
Artspoken Yardage
   (612) 222-2483
   Special effects, cloud and echo patterns
Cherrywood Fabrics, Inc.
   (218) 829-0967
   Suede-look cottons in gradations
Country House Cottons
   (319) 425-4384
   Solids, crushes, double-dipped cottons
Lunn Fabrics, Inc.
   (303) 623-2710
   Gradations, airbrushing, and more
Shades
   (800) 783-DYED
   Skies, mottled and streaked patterns
SkyDyes
   (203) 232-1429
   Hand-painted skies and naturescapes
Sonya Lee Barrington
   (415) 221-6510
   Gradations and marbled cottons

CUTTING THE PIECES

Pieced arcs usually contain two different wedges, illustrated as pieces D and E in **Diagram 1**. Note that wedge D has a right and left side, so the template is reversed to cut a mirror-image piece for one end of the arc.

To reduce fabric waste, like pieces can be traced side by side in long strips, as shown in **Diagram 3**. Since side edges are shared, this method will also speed the cutting time.

Stack and pin together multiple layers of fabric if you like, then cut through all layers at the same time with scissors. Be certain that wedges on all layers are cut accurately.

Diagram 3

Backgrounds (piece A) and melons (piece B) are often cut from the same fabric. Although their side edges cannot be shared, the templates can be positioned the way they are in **Diagram 4** to make the best use of your yardage.

Diagram 4

SEWING CURVED SEAMS

Most of the assembly procedures you'll encounter in Wedding Ring quilts involve matching curved seams. Center points are marked on the pattern pieces, so be sure to copy the points to your templates for easier matching. Also, to help you align pieces accurately, templates have been drawn to eliminate excess seam allowances at the points. The step-by-step directions below give information about successfully sewing the different types of curved seams you'll encounter. With a little practice, you'll be able to sew curves with confidence and ease.

Sewing Arcs to Melons

Step 1. Mark the center of each side of the melon and background pieces. If your quilt is made with solid rather than pieced arcs, mark the centers of the arcs, too. You may make a small mark with a pencil or fine-tip permanent pen. Or simply make a small snip at the center point with the tip of your scissors. Be careful not to cut deeper than 1/8 inch into the seam allowance. See **Diagram 5**.

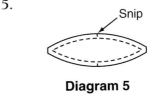

Diagram 5

Step 2. With right sides together, match the center of a melon to the center seam of a pieced arc, then pin at this point. See **Diagram 6A**. Match and pin the ends of the arc and melon. Place more pins along the seam if you like. See **6B**.

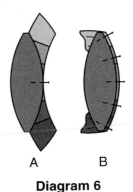

A   B

Diagram 6

Step 3. With the melon on top, sew the two pieces together using a 1/4-inch seam allowance. If you haven't pinned along the seam, manipulate the fabric with your fingers to fit the curve. Remove the pins as the needle approaches them. Press the seams toward the arc unless directed otherwise in the project instructions. Open out the melon piece, pressing the seam toward the arc unless directed otherwise. See **Diagram 7.**

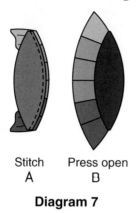

Stitch   Press open
A   B

Diagram 7

Step 4. Sew the pieced arcs with connecting wedges to the opposite or unsewn side of the melon. Match the center of the melon with the center seam of the longer arc and pin at that point. Then pin at each end. It is also helpful to place pins at the seam intersections at each end of the melon, matching the seams where the ends of the arc are sewn to the melon with the seams of the connecting wedges on the arc. See **Diagram 8A.**

Use a few more pins along the side, or simply manipulate the fabric with your fingers as you sew. Again, sew with the melon on top, using a ¼-inch seam allowance. It may be necessary to stop occasionally and reposition the fabric. If you do, be sure to stop with the needle down. Stitch all the way to the end of the arc. Open out the melon piece, pressing the seams toward the arcs unless directed otherwise. See **8B.**

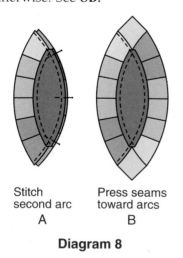

Stitch   Press seams
second arc   toward arcs
A   B

Diagram 8

Sewing Arcs to the Background

With right sides together, pin the center of one side of a background piece to the center of an arc/melon unit, with the background piece on top. Stick a pin in the background piece, ¼ inch from one end. Match that point with the seam on the arc between the connecting wedge and the next inner wedge of the arc. Repeat on the opposite end of the background piece. Add more pins along the length of the curve if you like. Sew the pieces together with a ¼-inch seam allowance. See **Diagram 9.**

Important: Start and stop your seams ¼ inch from each end, and backstitch. If you don't leave the ¼-inch seam allowance open, you won't be able to attach the arc/melon unit on the adjacent side.

Press the seams away from the arcs unless directed otherwise in the project instructions.

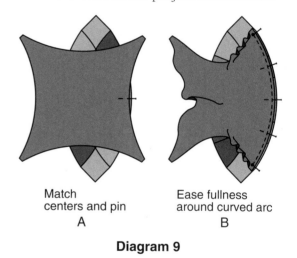

Match   Ease fullness
centers and pin around curved arc
A   B

Diagram 9

Sew Easy

To help ease your fabric along the curves, try clipping into the seam allowances on the concave curves. By making several small snips (no deeper than ⅛ inch) into the seam allowance, you'll give your fabric the flexibility to bend and manipulate around the convex curve of the melon to which you are attaching it.

Sewing Rings into Rows

Step 1. Sew additional arc/melon units to the quilt top following the project instructions. **Important:** When adding remaining arc/melon units, remember to match the seams where connecting wedges meet the rest of the arc, with the point ¼ inch from the tip of the background piece. Be sure to keep the ¼-inch seam allowance unsewn at the beginning and end of each curved seam.

Step 2. Once you have four arc/melon units coming together where four circles interconnect (see **Diagram 10**), you will need to stitch the connecting wedges together. To do so, match the raw edges of two adjacent connecting wedges and stitch from the edge to ¼ inch from the inner point where the wedges are connected to the arcs. Backstitch. Repeat for the other pair of wedges. Finger press the two seams you've just sewn in opposite directions, pin the remaining raw edges of the wedges together, and stitch, backstitching ¼ inch from each end. See **10B**.

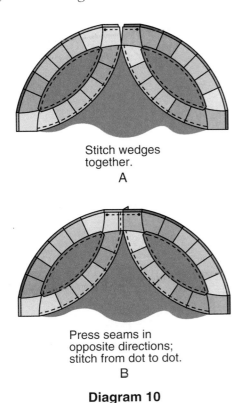

Stitch wedges together.
A

Press seams in opposite directions; stitch from dot to dot.
B

Diagram 10

Step 3. Sew the quilt top together as illustrated for your project, using the same techniques described here for aligning curves and finishing the connecting wedge seams.

APPLIQUÉING RINGS TO A BORDER

In a few projects in this book, the Wedding Ring quilt tops are appliquéd to a border unit or background. Any appliqué method will work for this step, but a freezer paper technique may help seam allowances stay in place easily.

Step 1. To make a stabilizing template for appliqué, connect the individual template pieces for the pieced arc, including the connecting wedges on opposite ends. Be sure you don't include seam allowances when constructing the shape of the complete arc. See **Diagram 11**.

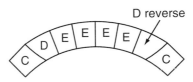

D reverse

C D E E E E C
C   C

Diagram 11

Step 2. Trace the shape onto the nonwaxy side of freezer paper and cut it out. Make a freezer paper template for each outer arc to be appliquéd.

Step 3. Align a freezer paper arc, waxy side up, to the wrong side of an outer pieced arc. The freezer paper should fit snugly against the inner seam allowance where the arc connects to the background piece. Use the tip of a medium-hot iron to press the outer seam allowance of the ring onto the freezer paper. See **Diagram 12**. This eliminates the need for basting or turning under edges as you work and holds the seam allowance securely as you appliqué the rings to the border.

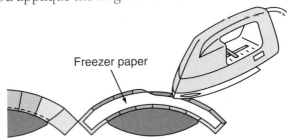

Freezer paper

Diagram 12

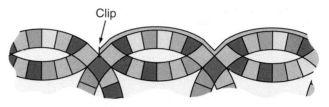

Diagram 13

Repeat, ironing a new freezer paper template onto each outer arc in your quilt. Construct the border and center the top on it, as described in the project directions. Appliqué the ring edges to the borders. Remove all freezer paper templates when the appliqué is complete.

BINDING CURVES

It is important that you use bias binding, which has more stretch, for quilts with curved outer edges. Refer to page 121 in "Quiltmaking Basics" for detailed information about making French-fold bias binding. You will need to make your bias binding 2 inches wide.

Step 1. To estimate the length of bias binding needed, measure around the perimeter of one outside arc. Multiply this measurement by the number of arcs around the outside of the quilt, then add 15 inches to the measurement. The calculation is the approximate number of inches of bias binding you will need.

Step 2. Begin sewing on the binding at the midpoint of a ring. With raw edges even, sew the binding around the curve, easing in the fullness. Do not stretch the binding to make it smooth.

Step 3. When you get to the inner point of two arcs, clip the seam allowance of the quilt for a flat fit, as shown in **Diagram 13**. Keep the needle down through all thicknesses of fabric, pivot at the inner point, and then continue stitching around the next curve, easing in the fullness of the binding.

Step 4. Continue sewing around each curve, clipping as necessary to help the binding turn at the corners. As you sew, make sure the portion of the quilt where binding has been attached is lying flat and is not buckled or puckered by binding that is pulled too tight.

When you have completed sewing the binding to the front of the quilt, fold the binding to the back of the quilt and stitch it in place by hand. As you near an inner point, fold the binding on one side of the point and stitch it to the inner corner. Then fold in the binding on other side of the corner. The binding will automatically form a miter. Continue hand stitching in place.

Treat outer, pointed areas of connecting wedges, such as those on the Is This Wedded Bliss? quilt, as you would a quilt corner, mitering each outer point as described in the binding instructions on page 122 in "Quiltmaking Basics."

WEDDING RING

Color Plan

Photocopy this page and use it to experiment with color schemes for your quilt.

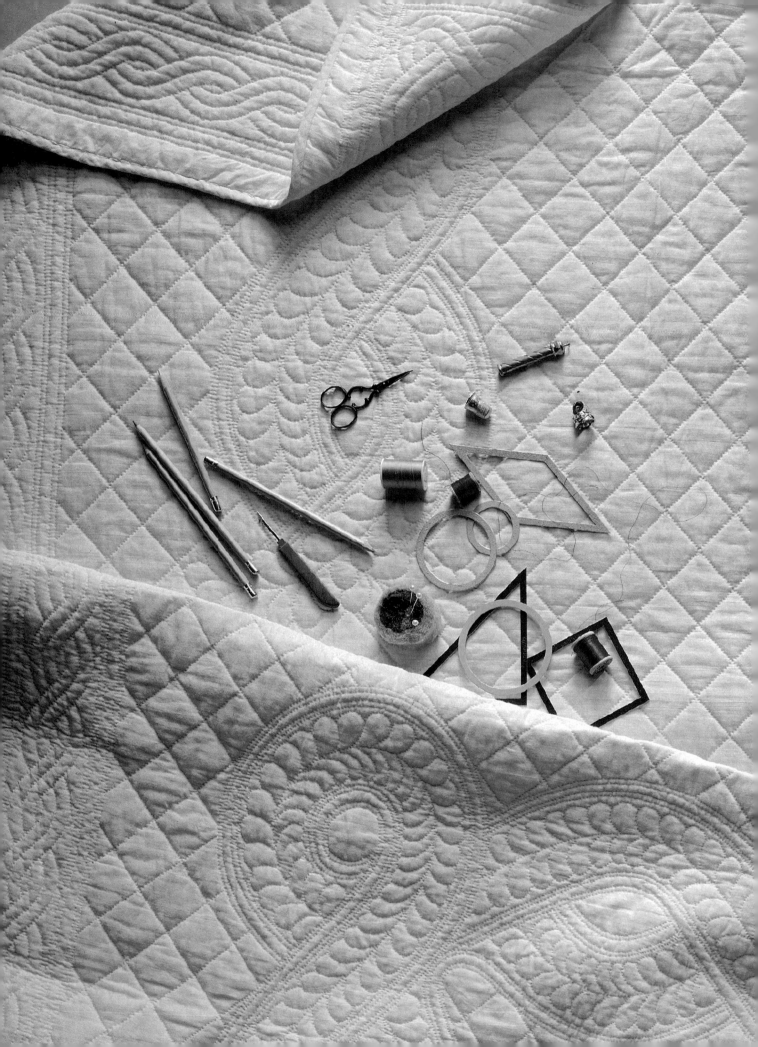

QUILTMAKING

BASICS

This section provides a refresher course in basic quiltmaking techniques. Refer to it as needed; it will help not only with the projects in this book but also with all your quiltmaking.

Quiltmaker's Basic Supply List

Here's a list of items you should have on hand before beginning a project.

• **Iron and ironing board:** Make sure these are set up near your sewing machine. Careful pressing leads to accurate piecing.

• **Needles:** The two types of needles commonly used by quilters are *betweens,* short needles used for quilting, and *sharps,* long, very thin needles used for appliqué and hand piecing. The thickness of hand-sewing needles decreases as their size designation increases. For instance, a size 12 needle is smaller than a size 10.

• **Rotary cutter, plastic ruler, and cutting mat:** Fabric can be cut quickly and accurately with rotary-cutting equipment. There are a variety of cutters available, all with slightly different handle styles and safety latches. Rigid, see-through plastic rulers are used with rotary cutters. A 6 × 24-inch ruler is a good size; for the most versatility, be sure it has 45 and 60 degree angle markings. A 14-inch square ruler will also be helpful for making sure blocks are square. Always use a special mat with a rotary cutter. The mat protects the work surface and helps to grip the fabric. Purchase the largest mat practical for your sewing area. A good all-purpose size is 18 × 24 inches.

• **Safety pins:** These are generally used to baste quilts for machine quilting. Use rustproof nickel-plated brass safety pins, preferably in size #0.

• **Scissors:** You'll need several pairs of scissors—shears for cutting fabric, general scissors for cutting paper and template plastic, and small, sharp embroidery scissors for trimming threads.

• **Seam ripper:** A seam ripper with a small, extra-fine blade slips easily under any stitch length.

• **Sewing machine:** Any machine with a straight stitch is suitable for piecing quilt blocks. Follow the manufacturer's recommendations for cleaning and servicing your sewing machine.

• **Straight pins:** Choose long, thin pins with glass or plastic heads that are easy to see against fabric so that you don't forget to remove one.

• **Template material:** Sheets of clear and opaque template plastic can be purchased at most quilt or craft shops. Gridded plastic is also available and may help you to draw shapes more easily. Various weights of cardboard can also be used for templates, including common household items like cereal boxes, poster board, and manila file folders.

• **Thimbles:** For hand quilting, a thimble is almost essential. Look for one that fits the finger you use to push the needle. The thimble should be snug enough to stay put when you shake your hand. There should be a bit of space between the end of your finger and the inside of the thimble.

• **Thread:** For hand or machine piecing, 100 percent cotton thread is a traditional favorite. Cotton-covered polyester is also acceptable. For hand quilting, use 100 percent cotton quilting thread. For machine quilting, you may want to try clear nylon thread as the top thread, with cotton thread in the bobbin.

• **Tweezers:** Keep a pair of tweezers handy for removing bits of thread from ripped-out seams and for pulling away scraps of removable foundations. Regular cosmetic tweezers will work fine.

Selecting and Preparing Fabrics

The traditional fabric choice for quilts is 100 percent cotton. It handles well, is easy to care for, presses easily, and frays less than synthetic blends.

The yardages in this book are generous estimates based on 44/45-inch-wide fabrics. It's a good idea to always purchase a bit more fabric than necessary to compensate for shrinkage and occasional cutting errors.

Prewash your fabrics using warm water and a mild soap or detergent. Test for colorfastness by first soaking a scrap in warm water. If colors bleed, set the dye by soaking the whole piece of fabric in a solution of 3 parts cold water to 1 part vinegar. Rinse the fabric several times in warm water. If it still bleeds, don't use it in a quilt that will need laundering—save it for a wallhanging that won't get a lot of use.

After washing, preshrink your fabric by drying it in a dryer on the medium setting. To keep wrinkles under control, remove the fabric from the dryer while it's still slightly damp and press it immediately with a hot iron.

CUTTING FABRIC

The cutting instructions for each project follow the list of materials. Whenever possible, the instructions are written to take advantage of quick rotary-cutting techniques. In addition, some projects include patterns for those who prefer to make templates and scissor cut individual pieces.

Although rotary cutting can be faster and more accurate than scissor cutting, it has one disadvantage: It does not always result in the most efficient use of fabric. In some cases, the method results in long strips of leftover fabric. Don't think of these as waste; just add them to your scrap bag for future projects.

Rotary-Cutting Basics

Follow these two safety rules every time you use a rotary cutter: Always cut *away* from yourself, and always slide the blade guard into place as soon as you stop cutting.

Step 1: You can cut several layers of fabric at a time with a rotary cutter. Fold the fabric with the selvage edges together. You can fold it again if you want, doubling the number of layers to be cut.

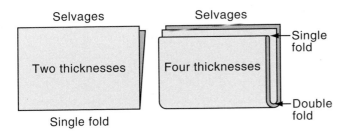

Step 2: To square up the end of the fabric, place a ruled square on the fold and slide a 6 × 24-inch ruler against the side of the square. Hold the ruler in place, remove the square, and cut along the edge of the ruler. If you are left-handed, work from the other end of the fabric.

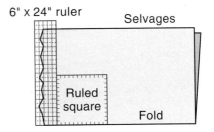

Step 3: For patchwork, cut strips or rectangles on the crosswise grain, then subcut them into smaller pieces as needed. The diagram shows a strip cut into squares.

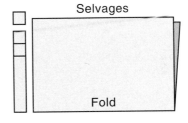

Step 4: A square can be subcut into two triangles by making one diagonal cut (A). Two diagonal cuts yield four triangles (B).

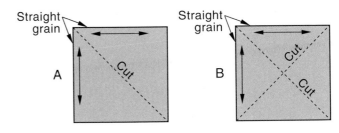

Step 5: Check strips periodically to make sure they're straight and not angled. If they are angled, refold the fabric and square up the edges again.

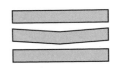

ENLARGING PATTERNS

Every effort has been made to provide full-size pattern pieces. But in some cases, where the pattern piece is too large to fit on the page, only one-half or one-quarter of the pattern is given. Instructions on the pattern piece will tell you where to position the pattern to continue tracing to make a full-size template.

MAKING AND USING TEMPLATES

To make a plastic template, place template plastic over the book page, trace the pattern onto the plastic, and cut out the template. To make a cardboard template, copy the pattern onto tracing paper, glue the paper to the cardboard, and cut out the template. With a permanent marker, record on every template any identification letters and grain lines, as well as the size and name of the block and the number of pieces needed. Always check your templates against the printed pattern for accuracy.

The patchwork patterns in this book are printed with double lines. The inner dashed line is the finished size of the piece, while the outer solid line includes seam allowance.

For hand piecing: Trace the inner line to make finished-size templates. Cut out the templates on the traced line. Draw around the templates on the wrong side of the fabric, leaving ½ inch between pieces. Then mark ¼-inch seam allowances before you cut out the pieces.

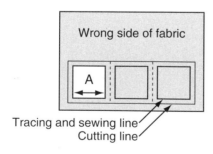

Wrong side of fabric

A

Tracing and sewing line
Cutting line

For machine piecing: Trace the outer solid line on the printed pattern to make templates with seam allowance included. Draw around the templates on the wrong side of the fabric and cut out the pieces on this line.

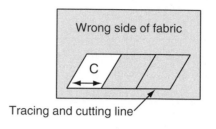

Wrong side of fabric

C

Tracing and cutting line

For appliqué: Appliqué patterns in this book have only a single line and are finished size. Draw around the templates on the right side of the fabric, leaving ½ inch between pieces. Add ⅛- to ¼-inch seam allowances by eye as you cut the pieces.

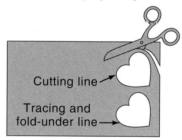

Cutting line

Tracing and
fold-under line

PIECING BASICS

Standard seam allowance for piecing is ¼ inch. Machine sew a sample seam to test the accuracy of the seam allowance; adjust as needed. For hand piecing, the sewing line is marked on the fabric.

Hand Piecing

Cut fabric pieces using finished-size templates. Place the pieces right sides together, match marked seam lines, and pin. Use a running stitch along the marked line, backstitching every four or five stitches and at the beginning and end of the seam.

When you cross seam allowances of previously joined units, leave the seam allowances free. Backstitch just before you cross, slip the needle through the seam allowance, backstitch just after you cross, then resume stitching the seam.

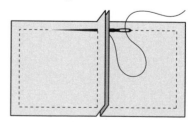

Machine Piecing

Cut the fabric pieces using templates with seam allowances included or using a rotary cutter and ruler without templates. Set the stitch length at 10 to 12 stitches per inch.

Place the fabric pieces right sides together, then sew from raw edge to raw edge. Press seams before crossing them with other seams, pressing toward the darker fabric whenever possible.

Chain piecing: Use this technique when you need to sew more than one of the same type of unit. Place the fabric pieces right sides together and, without lifting the presser foot or cutting the thread, run the pairs through the sewing machine one after another. Once all the units you need have been sewn, snip them apart and press.

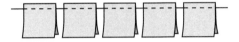

Setting In Pieces

Pattern pieces must sometimes be set into angles created by other pieces, as shown in the diagram. Here, pieces A, B, and C are set into the angles created by the four joined diamond pieces.

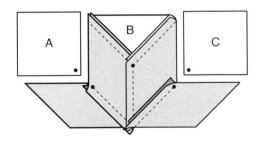

Step 1: Keep the seam allowances open where the piece is to be set in. Begin by sewing the first seam in the usual manner, beginning and ending the seam ¼ inch from the edge of the fabric and backstitching at each end.

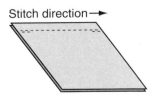

Step 2: Open up the pattern pieces and place the piece to be set in right sides together with one of the first two pieces. Begin the seam ¼ inch from the edge of the fabric and sew to the exact point where the first seam ended, backstitching at the beginning and end of the seam.

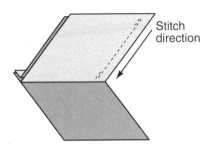

Step 3: Rotate the pattern pieces so that you are ready to sew the final seam. Keeping the seam allowances free, sew from the point where the last seam ended to ¼ inch from the edge of the piece.

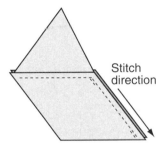

Step 4: Press the seams so that as many of them as possible lie flat. The finished unit should look like the one shown here.

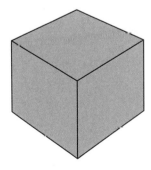

APPLIQUÉ BASICS

Review "Making and Using Templates" to learn how to prepare templates for appliqué. Lightly draw around each template on the right side of the fabric using a pencil or other nonpermanent marker. These are the fold-under lines. Cut out the pieces ⅛ to ¼ inch to the outside of the marked lines.

The Needle-Turn Method

Pin the pieces in position on the background fabric, always working in order from the background to the foreground. For best results, don't turn under or appliqué edges that will be covered by other appliqué pieces. Use a thread color that matches the fabric of the appliqué piece.

Step 1: Bring the needle up from under the appliqué patch exactly on the drawn line. Fold under the seam allowance on the line to neatly encase the knot.

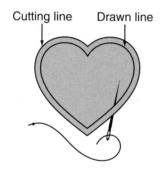

Cutting line   Drawn line

Step 2: Insert the tip of the needle into the background fabric right next to where the thread comes out of the appliqué piece. Bring the needle out of the background fabric approximately ¹⁄₁₆ inch away from and up through the very edge of the fold, completing the first stitch.

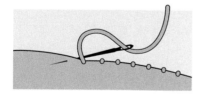

Step 3: Repeat this process for each stitch, using the tip and shank of your appliqué needle to turn under ½-inch-long sections of seam allowance at a time. As you turn under a section, press it flat with your thumb and then stitch it in place, as shown.

PRESSING BASICS

Proper pressing can make a big difference in the appearance of a finished block or quilt top. It allows patchwork to open up to its full size, permits more precise matching of seams, and results in smooth, flat work. Quilters are divided on the issue of whether a steam or dry iron is best; experiment to see which works best for you. Keep these tips in mind:

• Press seam allowances to one side, not open. Whenever possible, press toward the darker fabric. If you find you must press toward a lighter fabric, trim the dark seam allowance slightly to prevent show-through.

• Press seams of adjacent rows of blocks, or rows within blocks, in opposite directions. The pressed seams will fit together snugly, producing precise intersections.

• Press, don't iron. Bring the iron down gently and firmly. This is especially important if you are using steam.

• To press appliqués, lay a towel on the ironing board, turn the piece right side down on the towel, and press very gently on the back side.

ASSEMBLING QUILT TOPS

Lay out all the blocks for your quilt top using the quilt diagram or photo as a guide to placement. Pin and sew the blocks together in vertical or horizontal rows for straight-set quilts and in diagonal rows for diagonal-set quilts. Press the seam allowances in opposite directions from row to row so that the seams will fit together snugly when rows are joined.

To keep a large quilt top manageable, join rows into pairs first and then join the pairs. When pressing a completed quilt top, press on the back side first, carefully clipping and removing hanging threads; then press the front.

MITERING BORDERS

Step 1: Start by measuring the length of your finished quilt top through the center. Add to that figure two times the width of the border, plus 5 inches extra. This is the length you need to cut the two side borders. For example, if the quilt top is 48 inches long and the border is 4 inches wide, you need two borders that are each 61 inches long (48 + 4 + 4 + 5 = 61). In the same manner, calculate the length of the top and bottom borders, then cut the borders.

Step 2: Sew each of the borders to the quilt top, beginning and ending the seams ¼ inch from the edge of the quilt. Press the border seams flat from the right side of the quilt.

Step 3: Working at one corner of the quilt, place one border on top of the adjacent border. Fold the top border under so that it meets the edge of the other border and forms a 45 degree angle, as shown in the diagram. If you are working with a plaid or striped border, check to make sure the stripes match along this folded edge. Press the fold in place.

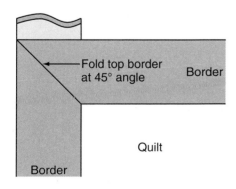

Step 4: Fold the quilt top with right sides together and align the edges of the borders. With the pressed fold as the corner seam line and the body of the quilt out of the way, sew from the inner corner to the outer corner, as shown in the diagram.

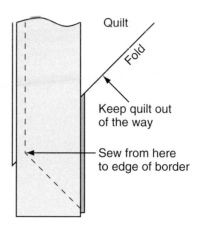

Step 5: Unfold the quilt and check to make sure that all points match and the miter is flat. Trim the border seam allowance to ¼ inch and press the seam open.

Step 6: Repeat Steps 3 through 5 for the three remaining borders.

MARKING QUILTING DESIGNS

To mark a quilting design, use a commercially made stencil, make your own stencil using a sheet of plastic, or trace the design from a book page. Use a nonpermanent marker, such as a silver or white pencil, chalk pencil, or chalk marker, that will be visible on the fabric. You can even mark with a 0.5 mm lead pencil, but be sure to mark lightly.

If you are using a quilt design from this book, either trace the design onto tracing paper or photocopy it. If the pattern will be used many times, glue it to cardboard to make it sturdy.

For light-color fabrics that you can see through, place the pattern under the quilt top and trace the quilting design directly onto the fabric. Mark in a thin, continuous line that will be covered by the quilting thread.

With dark fabrics, mark from the top by drawing around a hard-edged design template. To make a simple template, trace the design onto template plastic and cut it out around the outer edge. Trace around the template onto the fabric, then add inner lines by eye.

LAYERING AND BASTING

Carefully preparing the quilt top, batting, and backing will ensure that the finished quilt will lie flat and smooth. Place the backing wrong side up on a large table or clean floor. Center the batting on the backing and smooth out any wrinkles. Center the quilt top right side up on the batting; smooth it out and remove any loose threads.

If you plan to hand quilt, baste the quilt with thread. Use a long darning needle and white thread. Baste outward from the center of the quilt in a grid of horizontal and vertical rows approximately 4 inches apart.

If you plan to machine quilt, baste with safety pins. Thread basting does not hold the layers securely enough during machine quilting, plus the thread is more difficult to remove when quilting is completed. Use rustproof nickel-plated brass safety pins in size #0, starting in the center of the quilt and pinning approximately every 3 inches.

HAND QUILTING

For best results, use a hoop or a frame to hold the quilt layers taut and smooth during quilting. Work with one hand on top of the quilt and the other hand underneath, guiding the needle. Don't worry about the size of your stitches in the beginning; concentrate on making them even, and they will get smaller over time.

Getting started: Thread a needle with quilting thread and knot the end. Insert the needle through the quilt top and batting about 1 inch away from where you will begin stitching. Bring the needle to the surface in position to make the first stitch. Gently tug on the thread to pop the knot through the quilt top and bury it in the batting.

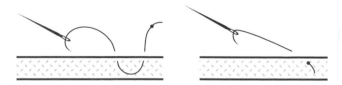

Taking the stitches: Insert the needle through the three layers of the quilt. When you feel the tip of the needle with your underneath finger, gently guide it back up through the quilt. When the needle comes through the top of the quilt, press your thimble on the end with the eye to guide it down again through the quilt layers. Continue to quilt in this manner, taking two or three small running stitches at a time.

Ending a line of stitching: Bring the needle to the top of the quilt just past the last stitch. Make a knot at the surface by bringing the needle under the thread where it comes out of the fabric and up through the loop of thread it creates. Repeat this knot and insert the needle into the hole where the thread comes out of the fabric. Run the needle inside the batting for an inch and bring it back to the surface. Tug gently on the thread to pop the knot into the batting layer. Clip the thread.

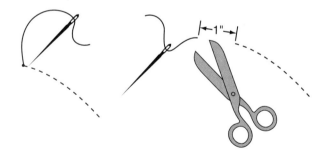

MACHINE QUILTING

For best results when doing machine-guided quilting, use a walking foot (also called an even feed foot) on your sewing machine. For free-motion quilting, use a darning or machine-embroidery foot.

Use thread to match the fabric colors, or use clear nylon thread in the top of the machine and a white or colored thread in the bobbin. To secure the thread at the beginning of a line of stitches, adjust the stitch length on your machine to make several very short stitches, then gradually increase to the regular stitch length. As you near the end of the line, gradually reduce the stitch length so that the last few stitches are very short.

For machine-guided quilting, keep the feed dogs up and move all three layers as smoothly as you can under the needle. To turn a corner in a quilting design, stop with the needle inserted in the fabric, raise the foot, pivot the quilt, lower the foot, and continue stitching.

For free-motion quilting, disengage the feed dogs so you can manipulate the quilt freely as you stitch. Guide the quilt under the needle with both hands, coordinating the speed of the needle with the movement of the quilt to create stitches of consistent length.

MAKING AND ATTACHING BINDING

Double-fold binding, which is also called French-fold binding, can be made from either straight-grain or bias strips. To make double-fold binding, cut strips of fabric four times the finished width of the binding, plus seam allowance. In general, cut strips 2 inches wide for quilts with thin batting or scalloped edges and 2¼ to 2½ inches wide for quilts with thicker batting.

Making Straight-Grain Binding

To make straight-grain binding, cut crosswise strips from the binding fabric in the desired width. Sew them together end to end with diagonal seams.

Place the strips with right sides together so that each strip is set in ¼ inch from the end of the other strip. Sew a diagonal seam and trim the excess fabric, leaving a ¼-inch seam allowance.

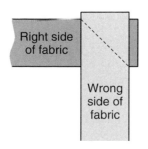

Making Continuous Bias Binding

Bias binding can be cut in one long strip from a square of fabric that has been cut apart and resewn into a tube. To estimate the number of inches of binding a particular square will produce, use this formula:

Multiply the length of one side by the length of another side, and divide the result by the width of binding you want. Using a 30-inch square and 2¼-inch binding as an example: 30 × 30 = 900; 900 ÷ 2¼ = 400 inches of binding.

Step 1: To make bias binding, cut a square in half diagonally to get two triangles. Place the two triangles right sides together as shown and sew with a ¼-inch seam. Open out the two pieces and press the seam open.

Step 2: Using a pencil and a see-through ruler, mark cutting lines on the wrong side of the fabric in the desired binding width. Draw the lines parallel to the bias edges.

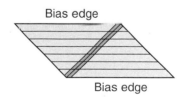

Step 3: Fold the fabric with right sides together, bringing the two nonbias edges together and off-setting them by one strip width (as shown in the diagram at the top of page 122). Pin the edges together, creating a tube, and sew with a ¼-inch seam. Press the seam open.

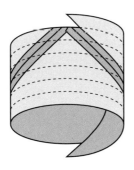

Step 4: Cut on the marked lines, turning the tube to cut one long bias strip.

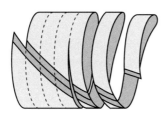

Attaching the Binding

Trim excess batting and backing even with the quilt top. For double-fold binding, fold the long binding strip in half lengthwise, wrong sides together, and press. Beginning in the middle of a side, not in a corner, place the strip right sides together with the quilt top, align the raw edges, and pin.

Step 1: Fold over approximately 1 inch at the beginning of the strip and begin stitching ½ inch from the fold. Sew the binding to the quilt, using a ¼-inch seam and stitching through all layers.

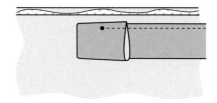

Step 2: As you approach a corner, stop stitching ¼ inch from the raw edge of the corner. Backstitch and remove the quilt from the machine. Fold the binding strip up at a 45 degree angle, as shown in the following diagram on the left. Fold the strip back down so there is a fold at the upper

edge, as shown on the right. Begin sewing ¼ inch from the top edge of the quilt, continuing to the next corner. Miter all four corners in this manner.

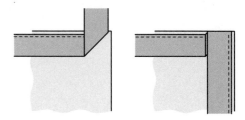

Step 3: To finish the binding seam, overlap the folded-back beginning section with the ending section. Stitch across the fold, allowing the end to extend approximately ½ inch beyond the beginning.

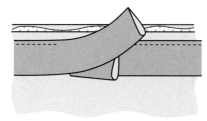

Step 4: Turn the binding to the back of the quilt and blindstitch the folded edge in place, covering the machine stitches with the folded edge. Fold in the adjacent sides on the back and take several stitches in the miter. In the same way, add several stitches to the miters on the front.

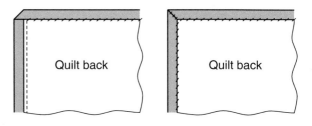

SIGNING YOUR QUILT

Be sure to sign and date your finished quilt. Your finishing touch can be a simple signature in permanent ink or an elaborate inked or embroidered label. Add any other pertinent details that can help family members or quilt collectors 100 years from now understand what went into your labor of love.